Help Yourself

Learn To
Produce, Publish & Promote
Your Book On Your Own

By Sybrina Durant

Edited by Christie Eilers

Help Yourself
Learn To Produce, Publish and Promote
Your Book On Your Own

Copyrighted 2015
Updated 2018

Paperback
ISBN-13: ISBN-13: 978-1512255836, ISBN-10: 1512255831
Ebook ISBN-13: 978-1-942740-03-2, ISBN-10: 1942740034
Paperback ISBN-13: 978-1-942740-02-5, ISBN-10: 1942740026

League City, Texas, United States of America

BISAC Codes:
LAN027000   LANGUAGE ARTS & DISCIPLINES / Publishing
REF026000   REFERENCE / Writing Skills
REF018000   REFERENCE / Questions & Answers

Disclaimer: This book will inform you what type of self-publishing information to look for and where to find it. It will guide you through major and minor steps required to produce (format), publish and promote or market your book on your own. By following the instructions, you will acquire the necessary information to produce, publish and promote your book by yourself for no cost. This book does not provide detailed instructions for using any particular word processing, graphics or any other type of program or tool. While the author does concentrate on particular programs and tools in this book, they are not the only tools available to you. Trademarked names are the property of their respective owners. This author claims no right to them. The information provided here is for educational purposes only. You are responsible for determining which programs and tools will work best for you and for learning to use any you decide to utilize. This author has purposely not provided screen shots from other companies in these instructions since doing so requires permission from each company. Please sign up with each website mentioned and log in so you may see the different screens while following the instructions provided. The major thrust of this book is to help you learn to help yourself successfully maneuver through the self-publishing process.

Contact Sybrina@sybrina.com.

This book is dedicated to:

...Paul Wuenschel....I was inspired to write this book, after he told me about his 80 year old mother, who was in the process of writing her own book. Learning about her, gave me the impetus to put as much as possible about what I've learned over the years into instruction book form so that my knowledge might easily be shared with her and others.

It is also dedicated to my much younger sister, who writes historical regency romance novels under the pen name of Gina Rose. I want her to have easy access to the production, publishing and promotion skills necessary to pursue her dreams...by herself...without my assistance long into her old age. Live long and prosper, dear sister.

This book is also dedicated to my longtime friend, Sandi Johnson. We began writing together thirty five years ago after meeting at a local writer's club event. That was long before self-publishing was even imaginable. Our paths crossed and diverged and met up again several times over the years. Over that time we both maintained our love of writing and our dreams of being successful at it. Recently, I vowed to do everything I could to help her get the bulk of her books formatted and published so that they would be available to the public for sale in Print-On-Demand (POD) and eBook formats. Now that that promise has been fulfilled, I'm referring her to this book so that she can do it by herself from now on. My hope is that lots of readers find and enjoy her children's books now that they are easily accessible to the public.

I hope the information imparted here, helps many aspiring authors attain their highest goals. It is never too late to begin to move towards achieving your most cherished dreams. And it is never too early, either. With that said, this final dedication is to my 7 grandchildren plus my nieces and nephews; and to all of the other bright young minds who've crossed my path. I pray all, who wish to, become prolific and successful self-published writers in their time. And I urgently encourage them to start while they're still young. Don't wait until tomorrow to start what you can start today. Finally, never forget: The written word is the greatest legacy anyone can leave to future generations.

GRATITUDE

This page is reserved for bestowing my most heartfelt thanks to the man who has made it possible for me to pursue my dreams.

Without his loving encouragement and support I would never have been able to "Help Myself" or any of the others whose lives have been changed because their dreams are now being further realized with each person who discovers one of their books.

Seeing the words one has worked so hard to perfect immortalized in print gives new hope and sense of purpose to an author.

Thank you, Marison Rice. Thank you for encouraging me to see how far I can go with my dream and for always being my biggest fan. It means the world to me.

Table of Contents for Help Yourself

Introduction

Dear Writer: Have you written a book? Would you like to offer it to the public for sale? Would you like to be able to do it all by yourself...for free? This book will show you how.

You might be wondering why I wrote this book. With all of the competition out there for writers, you might also be asking why I am willing to share all of my hard won information with others.

First of all, I'm not worried about the competition because everyone markets their particular book to their own sphere of influence. We each have just as much opportunity for sales as the next person. It all depends on how hard you want to work at it.

Many people have asked me how I know so much about the many things involved in producing (formatting and creating the book in physical, ebook or audio form), publishing (making the book available for sale to the public) and promoting (marketing and publicizing) books. When I try to explain it to them, I can see their eyes sort of glaze over. It all seems so complicated. And it is, if you don't know all of the steps to follow and in which order.

In one year, I produced and published nearly 30 books. That's a lot of books! The books which got published were children's picture books, illustrated books for teens, historical and regency romance novels and something I've decided to call Family Recollections books.

You can view 3 catalogs containing books I've published here -

http://www.sybrina.com/index_Sybrina_Publishing_Children_Stories_Retail_Catalog.htm

and here

*http://www.sybrina.com/index_Retail_Catalog_Regency_Rom
ance_by_Gina_Rose.htm*

and here

*http://www.sybrina.com/index_Family_Recollections_Books.h
tm*.

I accomplished all of that while working a full time job on the
side. (That last line was meant to be humorous but in
reality...for a while there...I did spend more time working on
publishing than I did at my "real job".)

Some of the books in those catalogs were written by me, some
by my sister, several by my longtime friend and one by my
mother-in-law.

Finally, my favorite book was written by my father. His dream
was to become a novelist. He pursued that dream into his late
70's, laying down memories from his past, hoping to share them
with his descendants. I wish he had lived long enough to see his
writings in published form but unfortunately his book was not
edited or published until years after he passed from this earth.
I am just grateful to the powers that be that I was able to
publish it posthumously so that future family members may
learn about their heritage in his words.

You can read more about it on my website at
http://www.sybrina.com/index_FRB.htm and if you have an
interest, you can purchase it on Amazon at
*http://www.amazon.com/Sad-Saga-1940s-America-
perceived/dp/1508995605*.

I took up the challenge of doing all of this work for my family
and friends simply because I knew how...and they didn't. It

seemed a lot easier to do it for them than to try to show or tell
them how to do it. After all, I hadn't written this book yet so I
had no step-by-step instruction document to share with them.

I learned a lot in that year of non-stop publishing and I've
refined many of the processes so that preparing a book for
publishing and actually publishing it is now a streamlined and
efficient work flow. There are very many steps involved in
producing, publishing and promoting a book. I wish I had come
across a book with all necessary instructions laid out in an easy
to follow step-by-step manner when I was first getting started.
It would have saved me so much misspent time and money and
a heck of a lot of frustration.

Once I had made it through the bulk of the backlog of books
that were waiting to be published for myself, friends and family
members, I decided there was no better time than the present
to compile this instruction book for them and for any other
budding writers who might want to know how to produce,
publish and promote their own books for FREE.

Yes, I said the word FREE. You can produce, publish and
promote your book on your own absolutely FREE of any cost to
you...except for the very low price of this ebook. This
instruction book will show you how to do it all by yourself.
There is nothing more beneficial than knowing how to "help
yourself". And nothing is more rewarding than learning how to
do so.

As I've worked on this book, the words I wrote for a song a very
long time ago have danced around in my brain again and again.
The lyrics were little pearls of wisdom that still apply today. The
title of the song is "Help Yourself".

I can't think of a more appropriate title for this book. As an
author, you must help yourself. You will not only be the writer,
but in most circumstances, you'll have to format the book

yourself. You'll have to publish it yourself and you will have to do all of the marketing and promotion by yourself, too.

A particular line of the lyrics has come back to me over and over, "No one can do...what you can do...for yourself". That is so true, but more appropriately, nobody WILL do for you what you will do for yourself. Sadly, no one is going to care about your ideas as much as you do. Even if someone takes enough interest in your book to help you along, it will still be up to you to get the message out (promote and market it).

You've got to believe in yourself. You must believe, deeply that your book has value for others. And you must work every day to that end.

I produced this instruction book to provide all of the necessary information to anyone interested in making a book ready for consumption by the public. Almost everyone I know knows someone who wants to write a book. The good news is, I can now share this book with them and with anyone else who wants to "write and publish their book"... like YOU. If you follow the instructions here, you will soon become an independently published author and you can immediately begin to promote your book to your sphere of influence and beyond.

You can produce (format), publish (make available to the public for sale) and promote (market) your book absolutely FREE of any cost to you. You will learn how to do that in this book.

All you need is a document that has been formatted in a word processing program like Microsoft Word for production purposes, a FREE account with CreateSpace for publishing and FREE accounts with Goodreads, Facebook, Twitter, Instagram and/or any of the many other social media sites available for promotion and marketing purposes. With these three things, you can absolutely present your book to the public for sale without having to spend a penny on anything unless you just want to.

Even if you don't have the means to purchase a word processing program...even if you can't afford an internet connection, you can still produce, publish and promote your book by yourself at no cost to you. Unknown to many is the fact that public libraries have public computers with Microsoft Office installed. They also offer internet use for their patrons. You can use their computers for free as long as you have a library card so there is really no excuse for not getting started on your book as soon as possible.

There are very many online publishing and distributing companies but most of their services are NOT FREE. CreateSpace is free. They will allow you to publish your book for FREE and then they will distribute it for FREE. The bulk of this book is going to center around getting your files prepared and uploaded to CreateSpace for publishing and distribution. CreateSpace is also affiliated with Amazon, so as soon as you have published your book through them, it will become available for purchase on Amazon and other online stores in

Print Format. After that, it is a very easy process to make it available in ebook form as well.

It wasn't very long ago that there were nearly no platforms available for individuals to publish and market their own books. Love them or hate them, CreateSpace and Amazon, together, have made the process of selling books to the world easy for the average everyday person. There are multiple benefits for offering your book to the public through Amazon. They will make the soft cover printed books available for purchase to customers on their websites all over the world and you'll be given the option to make a Kindle version of your book available for purchase there, as well. Both of those things are completely FREE to set up.

CreateSpace and Amazon do not charge you to set-up your book, nor do they charge you to be listed on their websites. But if you do sell any books through them, they will take a small percentage of the proceeds. That is only fair, though, considering everything else is FREE. Once you have a physical book and an ebook for potential customers to find on Amazon online stores, you can immediately start promoting and marketing it on social media.

Goodreads, Facebook, Twitter and Instagram are absolutely free sources for marketing books to the public. None of them charge membership fees or have yearly subscriptions. Goodreads has over 55,000,000 (that's 55 million) member readers who are looking for books to read. Those members catalog and rate books and share the ones they love with others. Some of those readers will write reviews about the books they have read.

There are also thousands of reading groups there, just like on Facebook. Joining and interacting with Goodreads and Facebook groups are the best ways to market your book. All groups allow you to post information, as long as it is related to the purpose of the group. All of this marketing is absolutely FREE to you.

You can do all of the above for FREE. However, if you want to offer your book in hard back or as an epub formatted ebook at other online stores such as Barnes and Noble or to online ebook distributors to libraries such as Overdrive, many other steps will be required and they WILL cost some money. If you desire to promote or advertise your book to other audiences besides social media sites, there are many options available that are not too cost prohibitive. You just have to know where to look. You will learn a lot about that in this book, also.

If you prefer to have help producing your book, there are very many reasonably priced services available for every aspect of book production and marketing from start to finish. You will learn what is available and how to find them in this book, too.

The ultimate goal of any author is to garner the attention of a big well known publisher and book distributor. There's no greater dream than seeing your book on the shelves of a neighborhood book store, a big chain book store or even at Walmart or Target!

Facts First...

The sad reality is that in most cases that is not going to happen. You are truly going to be on your own most of the way. You are going to have to help yourself get sales and most of the sales you do get are going to be from online bookstores, not physical book stores. There's a very logical reason for this.

The following figures are speculative and loosely based upon reports from Bowker (the world's leading provider of bibliographic information) and Wikipedia. It's not a stretch to say that in the United States alone, over 4,000 new books are offered to the public for sale - for the first time ever - each and every single day. That total is a combination of books released by Traditional publishers (304,912 titles in 2013) plus books released by Non-Traditional or Independent publishers (1,108,183 titles in 2013). That's 4,000 brand new books published every day, in just the United States. That doesn't begin to count what's being released every day in the rest of the world.

Consider that a moment. Nearly 1,500,000 new books are being released to the public for sale in this country each and every year. If every book ever published in the US alone, was available for sale in every book store in the country, these stores would be bigger than Walmarts or Targets! Heck! They'd be bigger than an entire shopping mall. It's no wonder only a select few books ever make it into a physical book store.

Even if you do manage to acquire a publishing contract with a traditional publishing company, there will never be a time for any author to just sit back and reap the rewards of fortune, fame and glory. In addition to anything a publisher may set up for you, they will still expect you to work very hard to market your book and yourself by yourself.

Most publishers will not take on an author who is not willing to spend their own time and effort to promote their own work. In fact, most publishers will only work with an author who has already managed to sell enough of their own books - on their own - to be profitable at it. And most publishing companies charge you every step of the way for every aspect of the entire process. That's right...they will all expect you to spend your own time and money marketing yourself.

I'm not telling you all of this to discourage you because I know it won't. After all, you are an author and you have something you want to share with the world. You have a story to tell or information you want to impart. Most writers are not doing it

for the glory anyway. They're writing because they have
something they want others to know or because they love to
share information. The best part about living in this day and
time is that everything is available to you right now, to do just
that via the internet. There are many ways to let people know
your book exists and many ways to get sales through the
internet. There are also many other avenues for selling printed
books such as book fairs or arts and crafts shows. Unlike in the
not too distant past, where only those authors who were either
in the right place at the right time or who knew somebody who
knew someone, writers today are free to go as far as they can
go by their own wits and grit. So "Help Yourself". If you want
to become a published author, nothing is stopping you but your
own initiative and drive. The extent of your success depends on
you.

Why Bother?

There are many reasons to become a non-traditional or
independent self-published author. The main reason is because
anyone can do it if they have the drive and desire. So, why not
you? There are many reasons to present your book to the
public for sale.

For instance:

Have you written the ultimate sci-fi story, love story, adventure
story or any other genre? Are you confident it contains proper
grammar and syntax? Then publish it! There's always an
audience for a good book.

Have you written lots of poetry? Compile your poems into book
form, categorizing them by year or season or love or grief and
any other category you can think of. Make it visually appealing
by adding an illustration for each poem. Publish the book so
others may purchase it for their own enjoyment.

Are you super crafty? Write a book with instructions for doing a particular project. Describe why the project interests you. Take photographs of each step along the way to the finished product. Have someone take pictures of you creating your masterpiece. Publish the book for all interested crafters to purchase. If you exhibit your wares at craft shows, you have the perfect audience for your book there, too!

Do you love making up recipes? Write a book featuring your best recipes. Have someone take pictures of you while you're working in the kitchen or picking herbs or vegetables from your own garden. Take pictures at events where the recipes are being enjoyed. Include rave reviews from people who love the recipes. Publish the book. People are always looking for new recipes to try out.

Are you a talented artist? Compile a book featuring your artwork with paragraphs of information on why you drew that picture or what you thought when you took that photo. Or turn your illustrations into children's stories. Or partner with a writer to bring your illustrations to life. Publish the book for the enjoyment of others.

Are you a successful business person with a unique business? Write your story detailing how you started your company. Let everyone know about your journey to success and offer tips on how they may be successful in that field, too.

Are you into genealogy? An actual book of family history makes a great gift for future generations. Illustrated books could be compiled for all of life's special events. Having a baby? Write a book for your baby about your pregnancy journey. Getting married? Write a book about planning the wedding, the ceremony, and the honeymoon. Have children? Start a book for each child. Once they can speak, ask them questions yearly and record their answers along with key photos. Give them the book when they move out to start their own lives.

Remember the life of a family member who has passed. – Ask
questions of parents, grandparents, aunts, uncles and others
while they are alive. Record their stories for descendants to
read years later. Include family photos, family trees and other
interesting collections from family members in the book.
Publish these Family Recollections books so they may be
purchased by future generations, years after today's relatives
have left this earth.

If there's a story or a book in you, then start your personal
journey writing, publishing and marketing. There's no better
time to start than now. Don't wait until tomorrow to start what
you can start today. Trust me, it's better to begin earlier rather
than later. Finally, never forget: The written word is the
greatest legacy anyone can leave to future generations. So get
busy!

Here's The Free Method

In order to produce a finished book for FREE, you must have access to a text editor. Even if you don't have a program like Microsoft Word yourself, in this day and time, it is highly likely that someone in your circle will be able to provide this tool to you. It certainly won't hurt to ask around. You may find that your friends and family will enjoy having the opportunity to work with you on your book project. Another possible option is to utilize the computers at the public library in your town. Most libraries have Microsoft Office programs on their public computers these days. Ask your librarian about that.

If you are producing a book that contains nothing but text, then Microsoft Word is a great tool. If you are producing an illustrated book, such as a poetry book with pictures or a cookbook or something similar, then you CAN also use Microsoft Word. It's the tool I used for this book. In fact, you can use Microsoft Word for any type of book except for one where you are trying to cover the entire page with an image - such as a children's picture book or an art or photography book. For that you will need to use a graphics program. My preferred graphics program is Microsoft Publisher. Once you have access to Microsoft Word or Publisher, then...

Sign up for a free account with CreateSpace.

As of this point in time, publishing a book through CreateSpace, which makes your book available on Amazon, is absolutely FREE. There are no production costs to the author at all. Go NOW to createspace.com and fill out all of the registration forms to set up a FREE account and you will be on your way to formatting and publishing your first book.

NOTE: *You must have a bank account in order to be paid by CreateSpace. You will have to provide your bank account information to them. You will also have to provide your social security number for tax filing purposes.*

Very important! *If you have a hyphenated last name, you must
list it that way on the CreateSpace registration forms. They will
report any income you happen to make from book sales to the
government. There's no getting around that. You will have to
include those sales in your tax preparation. But you also get to
report any expenses, too.*

After you have set up your CreateSpace author/publisher
account, you are ready to set up your first book title. You will
have to provide the Title of Your Book and names of all people
involved - (author(s), illustrator(s), and editor(s).

When prompted to select an ISBN number, choose "FREE
CreateSpace Assigned ISBN number". The next screen will list
both the 13 digit and 10 digit ISBN number formats. Copy and
paste both of those from that screen into your manuscript on
the Copyright Page.

NOTE: *In Microsoft Word, if you use Paste Special
|Unformatted Text, the text you copy from any source will come
in at the same size as the text in your document.*

The next CreateSpace webpage will prompt you to choose and
download a Microsoft Word template formatted to the size
your book will be. Make sure you download a template as it will
insure the book is formatted correctly to be published through
CreateSpace for the size of book you are planning to publish.
After you have done that, go ahead and exit CreateSpace. You
will log back into your CreateSpace account after you've
finished perfecting your book file.

TIP - At this point, you might want to consider purchasing a
small spiral notebook to begin keeping track of all of the
usernames and passwords you will be accumulating for the
book production, publishing and promotion process. The first
website info you'll enter into that notebook will be your
CreateSpace account information. Of course, you can also keep

track of everything on a jump drive or on your computer if you
wish. Whatever method you prefer is the best method for you
to use. Just do it for your own peace of mind. Now you're
ready to format your book.

Prepare Your Book

Produce the Book Interior

The very first decision to make is what size your book will be. You should have chosen the proper template size for your book when you began your book project in CreateSpace. Many different sized templates are available in Microsoft Word format through CreateSpace for the book interior. Use them for books with either no illustrations or for books with illustrations that do not need to extend to the edge of a page. They will be the best formatting tools for a CreateSpace project. Select one which works best for the presentation of your book. If you didn't do this when you created your CreateSpace Book project, do a search on your favorite search engine for CreateSpace interior template to quickly find the link for those templates.

You may "think" best into a pencil or do your most creative writing by hand. That is fine but any full text book will need to be typewritten before the formatting stage. You may type up your book using any text editor. But when it comes to formatting the book to the proper specifications, you must use a program which allows for all of the formatting required by CreateSpace. You can copy and paste text from any text editor into a CreateSpace template. Just make sure that you paste text with no formatting so that it won't mess up the formatting of the template. Make sure to name the book file "Book Title – Interior".

The interior of all books will include several elements. The front of a book needs to have a Title Page plus a separate page which contains 1) Copyright information, 2) ISBN information and 4) BISAC information, plus 4) some kind of statement of ownership and 5) maybe even a disclaimer.

Title Page

The Title Page will contain the book title, the author(s) name, editor(s) name (if any) and illustrator(s) name (if any). The title page for an illustrated book may also have a simplified picture or stylized text representing the book cover. Whether that illustration is black and white or color is a personal preference.

Note: *All of the example illustrations in the printed version of this book are in black and white. This was done purposely to keep production costs down. The hard cold truth is that is cost about 3 times more to print a book in color than to print it in black and white. If you wish to see the color illustrations you may find them in the ebook versions (Kindle and epub) of this book.*

Examples of Title Pages
Example 1-Romance Novel Title Page

Luther's Own

Book 3 From the Brother's In All Series

By

Gina Rose

Edited by Brian Cross & Sybrina Durant

Example 2-Children's Picture Book Title Page

Yarashell Abbily
and
Her Very Messy Room

Story by
Sybrina Durant

Illustrated by
Sara Wilson

Example 3 – *The Blue Unicorn's Journey To Osm*
Illustrated Book For Teens and Older Readers Book Title
Page

The Blue
Unicorn's

Journey
To
Osm

Illustrated Chapter Book

| Illustrated by | Written by | Edited by |
| Dasguptarts | Sybrina Durant | Kimberly Avery |

Example 4 – Family Recollections Book Title Page

My Dad's
House

Recollections captured by
Leona Rice

Edited By
Sybrina Durant

Copyright | ISBN | BISAC Page

The Copyright | ISBN | BISAC Page does not actually have to have
an official **Copyright Notice**. Once a book is published and
offered to the public for sale, that process automatically
"copyrights" a book. However, a line of copyright information
should absolutely be included. Something as simple as
Copyright 2017 by Publishing Company or Author Name is
sufficient.

Place the lines of information for this page in this order:

1) Book title at the top of the page
2) Copyright line
3) ISBN number or numbers
4) BISAC Codes
5) Publisher Information
6) The last section of information is the statement of
   ownership. A disclaimer can be included here.
7) The last line on this page may be an email address.

As I mentioned, you don't have to, but it is a really good idea to
register an official copyright after the book has been published
and made available for sale. Registering and providing
documentation can all be done online now.

NOTE: *As of 2017, the online copyright fee is $55.00 however,
the filing fee is $35 if you register one work, not made for hire,
and you are the only author and claimant. At the time of
registration, you will be prompted to upload a PDF copy of the
published book. The copyright website address is*
https://copyright.gov/registration/.

*Do not make the mistake of going to copyright.com. That is not
the government copyright office.*

NOTE: Another number which could be included on the Copyright|ISBN|BISAC page could be a LCCN or Library of Congress Control Number. This is not a Copyright number. It is a number of record that the Library of Congress uses to catalog books. It is the catalog record number, not the actual book number. The ISBN is the actual book number. There is a lot involved in the assignment of Library of Congress numbers.

Obtaining this number is free through the Library of Congress but you can purchase a LCCN number registration through CreateSpace if you wish. The current price for 2017 is $25.00 but with either method of application that you use, you must be aware that your book will NOT be guaranteed acceptance into the Library of Congress. Use the link below to begin the LCCN registration process.

https://www.createspace.com/Services/LCCNAssignment.jsp

It is not necessary to obtain an LCCN. I did go through the process for my first book, "Learn To Tie A Tie With The Rabbit And The Fox" but I never was able to track it down in the Library of Congress database so I have chosen not to continue that process for any more of my books. You can learn more about the uses and processes of LCCN, PCN, ISSN and other numbers at

http://www.loc.gov/publish/pcn/faqs/#control.

Then, you can decide for yourself whether to apply for them or not.

ISBN Number

All books offered to the public for sale in stores contain **ISBN Numbers** on the back of the book. It's also a good idea to list all associated ISBN numbers on the Copyright|ISBN|BISAC page. This is especially helpful to book stores or librarians who might want to order the book in different formats. The ISBN number identifies details about the book publisher and the pricing information for that edition. Each edition of a book should ideally have its own ISBN number. There should be one assigned for soft cover print, one for hard cover print, one for epub, one for audio and possibly others. When you set up your book through CreateSpace, you will be given the option to be assigned a FREE ISBN number through them. If you are publishing your book using the FREE method, then let CreateSpace assign the ISBN number. In fact, there are benefits to letting them assign the ISBN number no matter how you are publishing. One is that they will distribute your book to more re-sellers if you use their ISBN number.

ISBN numbers used to only contain 10 digits. In 2007, they increased to 13 numbers. The 13 digit number format is the preferred format displayed by most entities. In fact, if you received 10 digit numbers before 2007, there are ISBN number converters available for your convenience through Bowker and other sources. You may also use this one -
http://www.isbn.org/ISBN_converter

List the CreateSpace assigned ISBN number on the Copyright|ISBN|BISAC page. In Microsoft Word, make sure you use Copy | Paste Special | Unformatted Text because you do not want to make any mistakes in typing the number out. The 13 digit number must contain the dashes. If you wish, you may include a description that it is for a soft cover printed book. You may also list the book size in the ISBN number line. Unfortunately, you will not know the ASIN number for the Kindle book at this point, so you won't be able to list it at the time you publish the soft cover printed book. You may, however, include it after you've published the Kindle book.

NOTE: *An ASIN number is an Amazon Standard Identification Number used for Kindle ebooks and other products.*

Book Industry Standards and Communications (BISAC) Codes

BISAC codes are now required by both public and school librarians to make it easier for them to determine where to shelve books. Most bookstores require BISAC codes also because it makes it easier to shelve books by genre. BISAC Codes must be listed at the top left corner on the back of the book cover. List all of the BISAC Codes you have chosen there and also on the Copyright | ISBN | BISAC page of the book. CreateSpace allows you to list 3 different BISAC codes in their database.

In fact, if you don't list BISAC codes for your book on their website, you will not be allowed to distribute your book through the CreateSpace Expanded Distribution Service. There are categories and sub-categories of every book genre imaginable on the Book Industry Study Group (BISG) website. You can drill down as narrowly as you wish or chose as broad a code as you want. These codes will become part of the metadata for your book as they are directly related to search engine results.

Some sample BISAC codes are:

JUV000000	JUVENILE FICTION / General
JUV012030	JUVENILE FICTION / Fairy Tales & Folklore / General
FIC027070	FICTION / Romance / Historical / Regency
FIC051000	FICTION / Cultural Heritage
EDU024000	EDUCATION / Reference
TRV026000	TRAVEL / Special Interest / General
CKB021000	COOKING / Courses & Dishes / Cookies
CRA055000	CRAFTS & HOBBIES / Knots, Macramé & Rope Work

There are literally hundreds of categories. To learn more about BISAC codes, go to *http://bisg.org/page/bisacedition* . **Not**e: BISG is a pretty expensive membership only organization and sometimes, they will change their web addresses. If you use the link above and you arrive at an error page, simply search for "list of bisac codes" on your favorite search engine. For more information about bisac codes, read this - *http://www.ingramspark.com/blog/bisac-subject-codes*

Publisher Information

If you are going to independently publish books, I recommend that you come up with a company name for your publishing company. If you use something as simple as "Your Name Books" you don't really have to register the name with any government agency. As long as you identify yourself as "Sole Proprietor" on any business forms you may simply use your social security number as your tax number.

Note 1: If I had it to do over again, I wouldn't use my name in the name of my book publishing company. I'm beginning to realize it would look more professional when trying to market and promote my books if it appeared as if a separate entity was the publishing company. Just something to think about...

Note 2: If you decide that you would like to protect yourself further regarding taxes, you might want to register your company name with your county clerk as a DBA (Doing Business As). You can gain even further protection by setting up an LLC (Limited Liability Company). Read a great article about that here - ***https://kindlepreneur.com/how-to-start-a-publishing-company***

It is important to include your publishing company information on the Copyright|ISBN|BISAC page. At a minimum, include your publishing company name, email address, city, state and country. You do not have to list your street address. Listing your email address is a very, very good idea as you want to encourage people to reach out to you.

Statement of Ownership or Permission Statement

The Copyright | ISBN | BISAC page of the book should contain a statement about the reservation of rights similar to this: "All rights reserved by Publishing Company name. This book contains material protected under International and Federal Copyright Laws and Treaties. Any unauthorized reprint or use of this material is prohibited. No part of this book may be reproduced or transmitted in any form or by any means, electronic or mechanical, including photocopying, recording, or by any information storage and retrieval system without express permission from the publishing company." The statement doesn't have to be that elaborate. Read those written in books you already have and put together something that works for you.

Disclaimer

If you are writing a book about real people, you will definitely want to include a disclaimer stating some variation on several of the thoughts below:

1) The memories of our lives are our own. Not everyone will agree with all of those memories.
2) The writings found within this book could appear to, or actually will contain errors.
3) No two people ever remember the same situation in exactly the same way.
4) This book was not necessarily written to represent word-for-word transcripts.
5) The author speaks with a voice that evokes the feelings and meanings of remembered events.
6) The words on the pages are simply the recollections and memories of one family member and possibly one or more other people.

7) The information on these pages should not be compared to that found on genealogy sites. This book is not to be confused with traditional genealogy efforts which may require proof of sourcing, indexed records, degrees of certainty, footnoting, census records and other official documentation.

8) This book may best be considered a work of creative non-fiction. Everything in it is true (to the best of one's recollection) if not entirely factual, and nothing is so far from the truth as to be considered fiction. Human memory, after all, can be deeply flawed.

9) Minor details and even some major aspects of a situation might have been forgotten or remembered differently over time but the main point is that it has been remembered and captured by the person providing the details to the rest of the family.

There are many websites which offer examples of disclaimers or permission statements. Do a little research to determine how you want to word yours.

Examples of Copyright|ISBN|BISAC Page
Example 1-Romance Novel Copyright Page

Luther's Own

Copyrighted 2014

Paperback
ISBN-13: 978-1508570196, ISBN-10: 1508570191
Ebook ISBN-13: 978-0-9906537-8-3,
ISBN-10: 0990653781
Paperback ISBN-13: 978-0-9960940-9-2,
ISBN-10: 0996094091

BISAC Codes:

FIC027000 FICTION / Romance / General

FIC027070 FICTION / Romance / Historical / Regency

All rights reserved by Sybrina Publishing and
Distribution Company.

League City, Texas, United States of America

This book contains material protected under
International and Federal Copyright Laws and
Treaties. Any unauthorized reprint use of this
material is prohibited.

No part of this book may be reproduced or
transmitted in any form or by any means,
electronic or mechanical, including photocopying,
recording, or by any information storage and
retrieval system without written permission from
Sybrina Publishing and Distribution Company.

Contact Sybrina@sybrina.com.

Example 2-Children's Picture Book Copyright Page

"Yarashell Abbily and Her Very Messy Room"

Story copyright 3/2014

Soft Cover Print ISBN-13: 978-0-9960940-0-9, ISBN-10: 0-9960940-0-8
Soft Cover Print ISBN-13: 978-1499504125, ISBN-10: 1499504128
Ebook ISBN-13: 978-0-9960940-1-6, ISBN-10: 0-9960940-1-6
Hard Cover ISBN: ISBN-13: 978-0-9960940-3-0, ISBN-10: 0996094032

BISAC Codes:

JUV000000— JUVENILE FICTION / General
JUV013060—JUVENILE FICTION / Family / Parents
JUV013000—JUVENILE FICTION / Family / General
JUV040000—JUVENILE FICTION / Girls & Women
JUV057000—JUVENILE FICTION / Stories in Verse

Example 3-Family Recollections Book Copyright Page

My Dad's House

Story Copyright 11/2014

Soft Cover Print ISBN-13: 978-1503259461,
ISBN-10: 1503259463

BISAC Codes: FAM000000 - Family and Relationships—General
HIS000000 - History—General

This book may best be considered a work of creative non-fiction.
Everything in it is true (to the best of one's recollection) if not entirely
factual, and nothing is so far from the truth as to be considered fiction.
Human memory, after all, can be deeply flawed. Minor details and even
some major aspects of a situation might have been forgotten or
remembered differently over time but the main point is that it has been
remembered and captured by the person providing the details to the rest
of the family.

Contact Sybrina@sybrina.com.

Example 4-Historical Novel Copyright Page

A Sad Saga of 1940's America

How a 10 year old boy perceived events...

Copyrighted 2015

Paperback ISBN-13: 978-1508995609, ISBN-10:
1508995605
Ebook ISBN-13: 978-0-9960940-8-5, ISBN-10:
0996094083
Paperback ISBN-13: 978-0-9906537-9-0, ISBN-10:
099065379X

BISAC Codes:
FIC000000 FICTION / General
FIC002000 FICTION / Action & Adventure
FIC008000 FICTION / Sagas

All rights reserved by Sybrina Publishing and
Distribution Company.

League City, Texas, United States of America

This book contains material protected under
International and Federal Copyright Laws and
Treaties. Any unauthorized reprint use of this
material is prohibited.

No part of this book may be reproduced or
transmitted in any form or by any means,
electronic or mechanical, including photocopying,
recording, or by any information storage and
retrieval system without written permission from
Sybrina Publishing and Distribution Company.

— Contact Sybrina@sybrina.com.

Additional Optional Pages

Some additional optional pages that you might want to add to
the front of the book could include Table of Contents,
Dedication Page, Introduction, Cast of Characters, Maps and/or
other pages of your choosing.

After the book content - many books contain Indexes, Author
Profiles, Letter to Readers or even Sales or Advertising pages
containing information about other books that the author or
publishing company has published.

These are perfectly acceptable for self-published books, but do
not put any pricing information on the sales sheets as they may
change from online store to online store and prices will certainly
vary at brick and mortar stores. For books published through
CreateSpace, do not provide sales links to any other book selling
sites that are in competition with Amazon, either. You
absolutely can place web addresses to your own website or
blog, though.

Another type of page which might be included at the back of a
book could be a Song Lyrics page. Many children's books (and
other types of book like this one) have accompanying songs
these days. Remember to include links to where the songs may
be heard for free or purchased.

It's also a great idea to provide a page with Facts about the
subject matter of the book. These could be historical facts,
scientific facts, or any other information regarding the subject.

Last but not least, if you sell any book related merchandise like
hats or t-shirts or trading cards, be sure to include a Book Loot
page.

Examples of Optional Pages

Example 1-Dedication Page from the front of "Yarashell Abbily and Her Very Messy Room"

Example 2-Dear Reader Page from the back of "Learn To Tie A Tie With The Rabbit And The Fox"

Dear Reader:

If you and your child enjoyed "Learning to Tie a Tie with the Rabbit and the Fox", please take a moment to write a positive review on the site where you found this book.

As an independent author, my book sales are almost completely dependent on satisfied readers like you, spreading the message to others. Your kind words will be greatly appreciated.

And please don't forget to let potential readers know how much you enjoyed the artwork by Donna Marie Naval.

Thank you for your support,

Sybrina@Sybrina.com

**_Example 3_-About the Author Page from the back of the
romance novel "Luther's Own" – Book 3 of the Brothers In
All Series**

Gina Rose

ABOUT THE AUTHOR

My father was a great story teller and always
said that one day, he would like to write a novel.
My sister is a writer as well, so naturally I'm a
dabbler. I thought I'd try my hand at writing
romance novels because I love to read them.
Romance novels have everything you want,
mysteries, villains, wonderful character's and I
easily find myself living in the moment with the
story. I hope that readers will find my stories as
entertaining as I have found so many. I like to mix
tragedy and comedy together with a cast of colorful
characters that I create from people that I have met
in my life. I will visualize a person that I know as
this or that character and the rest is history.

I hope you enjoy my warped sense of humor and
the stories that I tell. If you happened upon this
book first, please go back and read My Sweet
Alyssa, the first of the Brother's In All series and
Resurrecting Dylan, the second book of the series.

Gina Rose is the pseudonym for a very prolific author
who spins tales in the Regency Romance genre.

Look for many more or her books to be available soon
on Amazon and most other online bookstores.

Check her website, ginarose-author.com, often for
more information and reviews.

Example 4-Song Lyrics Page from the back of "Nellie Knows How To Knot A Neck Scarf"

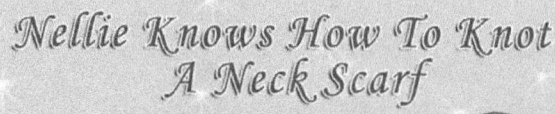

Nellie Knows How To Knot A Neck Scarf
Song Lyrics

Nellie knows, Nellie knows.
Listen closely, then you'll know
How to knot a neck scarf
With the rabbit and the fox.

Rabbit ran around the tree.
Fox was close behind.
Round the tree they ran again
One more time.

Oh where could Rabbit hide?

Then, quick under a bush, the little Rabbit fled
Only keeping one step ahead.
Then, Rabbit took a giant leap
And he barely cleared
The top of a big round log.

That poor Fox...

He could only watch
As the Little Rabbit dove
To the safety of his cool dark hole.

Nellie knows, Nellie knows.
If you listened closely, now you know
How to knot a neck scarf
With the rabbit and the fox.

Listen to this song for FREE at Sybrina.com

Example 5-Cast of Characters Page from the front of the illustrated book for pre-teens - "Legend of the Blue Unicorn"

Cast of Characters

Blue / Osm—A plain blue unicorn who has been born into the Tribe of the Metal Horn. All other unicorns in the tribe have magical metal horns, but not him. This story is about his quest to find his own magic. His future mate is Ghel.

Alumna—A pale rose colored, gypsy like unicorn, with an aluminum horn. She is the tribe's sooth-sayer. Her magical powers allow her to peer into a crystal ball to see into the future and the past. Her mate is Iown.

Silubhra—A white unicorn who is very kind to Blue. She is very emotional and her white coat turns dark pink when she's angry. Her silver horn gives her the most beautiful silvery musical and persuasive voice. Her mate is Nix.

Ferrum—A green unicorn who has a brass horn. He has lemons and limes in his hair. He can imitate the sound of any brass musical instrument with his horn and provides a lot of entertainment for the tribe. His mate is Style.

Style—A purple unicorn who runs the Mane-Do salon. She uses her steel horn to style all of the unicorn manes into magical creations. Her mate is Ferrum.

Lauda—An elderly dark gray unicorn with a lead horn. She is the book keeper of the tribe. She is the recorder of history and is rather stern. Iown is her mate.

Iown—A black unicorn and the eldest of the tribe. He is a philosopher who is quiet and thoughtful, with an iron horn and an iron will. Everyone trusts Alumna's mate to give them good advice.

Ghel—A golden unicorn with a heart of gold, as well. She is Alumna's assistant and is learning the arts of sooth-saying. She also works with Dr. Zinko in the healing room. She is Blue's future mate.

Nix—The head of Unicorn Defense. The red unicorn is responsible for the security of the Hostable. He uses his nickel horn to nix any disaster in the nick of time. His mate is Silubhra.

Dr. Zinko—The doctor of the tribe wears a green coat. His zinc horn allows him to quickly heal all kinds of ills. He handles the well being of everyone and maintains the Healing room. His mate is Lauda.

Tinam—The chef of the tribe is a yellow unicorn. His tin horn gives him the ability to magically preserve food in little tins that open up to be piping hot delicious meals. His mate is Cuprum.

Cuprum—An orange unicorn who runs the Water Facilities in the Hostable. Her copper horn gives her the power to magically transform dirty water into clean water.

Example 6-Additional Books for Sale Page at the back of "Learn To Tie A Tie With The Rabbit And The Fox"

Sybrina Publishing

Exercises in manual dexterity build self-esteem in children. Knowing how to tie shoe-strings, neckties, scarves or any other knot is a useful and rewarding skill. But it can be quite challenging to master. Sybrina Durant takes the seemingly complicated task of tying a necktie knot and makes it fun and simple for both boys and girls. Her charming "Rabbit and the Fox" series of books will delight children and their parents. These books are not meant to be passive reads. Kids are encouraged to grab a tie or scarf and while reading, use it to follow the moves of the fox chasing the rabbit through the forest. The satisfying end result of this stimulating activity is a neatly knotted necktie or scarf. For a great bonding experience, get the whole family involved in learning how to tie!

ISBN# 978-0-9960940-2-3 (SC)   ISBN# 978-0-9729372-7-6 (SC)   ISBN# 978-0-9729372-5-2 (SC)

ISBN# 978-0-9729372-3-8 (HB)   ISBN# 978-0-9906537-0-7 (HB)   ISBN# 978-0-9906537-1-4 (HB)

Visit Sybrina.com to learn where to buy the books in all soft cover or hard back print formats. Listen to the accompanying song there!

ISBN# 978-0-9891572-2-3(SC)   ISBN# 978-0-9906537-6-9 (SC)

ISBN# 978-0-9906537-4-5 (HB)   ISBN# 978-0-9906537-7-6 (HB)

Visit http://
www.sybrina.com/
index_Sybrina_Publishing_
Children_Stories_Retail_
Catalog.htm to view entire
children's book catalog from
Sybrina Publishing.

Books may immediately be purchased at any online bookstore in soft cover (SC) or hardback (HB). They are also available in all electronic formats. Visit Sybrina.com to access links for purchasing the books from stores . Note: If the books are not available on store or library shelves, they may be requested from any bookstore or library associate. Just provide the ISBN number for any book format listed above to a store clerk or librarian and they will order the books. Bonus! Listen to the Rabbit and the Fox song at Sybrina.com in English, Spanish or Tagalog. You'll find yourself singing right along.

Example 7 – Sales Page from the backs of Children's Books by Sandi Johnson, Britt Brundige and Sybrina Durant

Children's Books Presented To You By The Following:

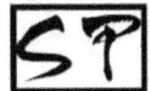 Contact:
Sybrina@
sybrina.com

Sybrina Publishing

 Little Choo Choo Books

Moon-Star Stories

Contact:
Sandi@
Dorpexpress.
com

**All of these books are available at Amazon.com in print and Ebook formats.
Ask for them at your local library and your favorite book stores.
For discount price information contact Sybrina or Sandi.**

**Visit Sybrina.
com for more
info about all of
these books by
Sandi Johnson,
Britt Brundige
and Sybrina
Durant.**

**More
Books
Coming
Soon!**

**All of these books have accompanying songs. Listen to them for FREE at
http://www.reverbnation.com/dorpexpress/ or Sybrina.com.**

Example 8-Facts Page from the back of Sandi Johnson's "Book 6 – Dorp The Scottish Dragon – A Lone Star Story"

SOME INTERESTING TEXAS FACTS

There are many interesting facts about the Lone Star State of Texas .Things to remember are :

1. Long Horn Steers are the official large mammal of Texas.
2. Armadillos are the official small mammal of Texas.
3. Bluebonnets are the state flower. It is against the law to remove them from the land where they grow.
4. The city of Houston was named after the famous general, Sam Houston.
5. A woman named Charlotte Allen convinced her husband to purchase the land that would become Houston, Texas.
6. Houston is the largest city in the great state of Texas.
7. Houston was built on a mosquito infested swamp, next to a prairie full of red ant hills.
8. Tornadoes, in Texas, are called twisters.
9. There are lots of prickly cactus in Texas. Don't fall into one or you may need a pair of tweezers!
10. The word "rodeo" means round-up.
11. The very first rodeo in the United States was held in Pecos, Texas in 1883.

Example 9-Index Page from the back of "Sybrina's Phrase Thesaurus – Volume 3 – Physical Attributes"

Example 10-*Merchandise Page From "The Blue Unicorn's Journey To Osm Illustrated Book For Teens"*

Find Trading Cards, T-Shirts, Mugs and Other Unicorn Bling and Book Swag like those pictured below at https://www.zazzle.com/collections/journey_to_osm-1195575554153312638

Trading Cards for Each Unicorn

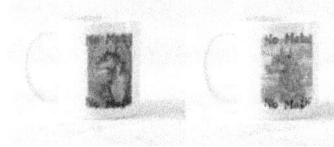

T-Shirts for Each Unicorn

Mugs for Each Unicorn

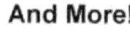

Stickers for Each Unicorn

And More!

Book Content

The content of any book is totally at the discretion of the writer
and limited only by the imagination. Book content may simply
be text or it may include illustrations. There is nothing much I
can do to guide you with that creative process. You are on your
own there. The main thing is - Don't let anyone tell you that
you can't write about this or that. The thought police seem to
have taken over the world these days and it can be daunting to
consider facing up to a possible onslaught of mean words from
people who disagree with you. If you have something to say
that you feel needs saying...If you can think it, you can put it on
paper. Don't be afraid to dream or to put your own experiences
in writing. Strangely enough, sometimes, the worst critiques
from the most insulting critics are the ones that actually sell the
books.

Beta Readers

Before you think about publishing or even having your book
edited, you might want to consider getting the opinion of some
other readers to see if there is anything you might have missed -
or based on their suggestions that you might want to change in
your book. Luckily there are armies of people out there who
will read and give their opinion on different aspects of all
different kinds of books.

Gaining their attention might take a little work on your behalf
but you can start out by joining different Facebook groups
dedicated to this purpose. Find them by doing searches on
words like "Street Team" "Beta Readers" or "ARC Readers" -
ARC = Advanced Reader Copies.

Be aware that you will be expected to give an electronic copy of
your book to these readers. Do not expect them to purchase
your book from you as they are providing a valuable service to
you for free. Some will even suggest or do some editing for you.

Book Editing

Self-published authors can find themselves under much greater
scrutiny by reviewers and readers than traditionally published
authors. That is why it is especially important to ensure your
writing is the best it can possibly be before the outside world
sees it. There are many things which will draw negative
attention from readers. Two that particularly stand out for me
are the misuse of tense (present or past) or an overly-generous
sprinkling of particular words throughout a story.

You can read a fantastic article on the use of past or present
tense at this link.
*http://theeditorsblog.net/2012/01/31/narrative-tense-right-
now-or-way-back-then/*

Before publishing, it is essential to edit your document for any
unnecessary, superfluous or over-used words. What are some
of these offending words? This, that, just, and, then, very, only
are just a few. There are actually many, many more that can
jump off a page and thoroughly interrupt a reader's enjoyment
of a story. If you use Microsoft Word, you could use the Find
tool to enter each word and then go through a very lengthy
process to remove or change these words.

Even better, in Word, you have access to a very handy feature in
the Find and Replace tool, which will make the process
practically painless versus using the Find tool alone. Just click
on the Replace button under Editing on your Home tool tab.
Once there click the Find tab and enter one of your offending
words. Then, click the Reading Highlight button and select
Highlight All.

I did that for the sentence below. As you can see, every
instance of the word "that" has been highlighted in yellow.

"This and that, this and that, this and that," said the rat.

Now, it is very important to note here that the yellow
highlighting will not stick if you start editing. There is a fix for
this. In the "Replace with field", enter ^& by itself. Click the
format button at the bottom of the Find and Replace tool
window and select Highlight. Finally, click the Replace All
Button. The highlighting will stick until you click on the Text
Highlight Color button (under the Home tab) and change it to
No Color.

An even better method of finding these offending words is to
use a Macro for Word called the Needless Words Macro. You
can get it free at ***http://www.techtoolsforwriters.com/omit-
needless-words-with-a-macro/*** along with complete
instructions for installing it and modifying it. It will do all the
work of highlighting many different words that might need to
be omitted all at the same time. It's much easier than the
"searching for one word at a time" method. There are many
useful tools listed in the article. Another good article on the
subject is ***http://www.beyondpaperediting.com/how-to-
improve-your-writing-with-macros-tips-for-beginners/*** .

I can't stress enough times how absolutely essential it is to have
your book edited by someone else besides youself before you
upload it to CreateSpace. It is nearly impossible for a book
creator to capture every single error in a completed manuscript.
Your eyes simply become blinded after looking at the same
thing over and over again. Fresh eyes are absolutely necessary.
Of course, a professional editor is the best choice but you don't
have to go there.

For the FREE method of publishing, reach out to a friend or
family member for help with this step of the book. If you feel
confident about the content of the book, just ask them to mark
the book up to show you where you've overused certain words
like "and" or "that" or to note if you're misusing past and
present tense. They will notice if there are duplicate words or
paragraphs. They will also ask questions about things you might

not have thought about, perhaps allowing you to enhance the book content. Let them know you value their input and someone will be happy to help.

Upload The Book Interior File To CreateSpace

Once the content of the book is finalized, you will need a file containing only the books interior for uploading to CreateSpace. If your book is mostly text (such as a novel of some sort) or even if it contains some illustrations but none that extend beyond the edges of the pages (such as for a children's picture book), you may (and should) upload a Word doc to CreateSpace.

You may even, later, upload this same Word Doc to be converted to Kindle. If the uploaded file is for a novel, no special considerations for file formatting will need to be applied. However, if it is for a book containing some illustrations, you should make a few modifications to the word doc so that it will look as good as possible as a Kindle ebook.

When a Word doc is used to convert your book file to Kindle, it gives the reader the ability, in Kindle, to make the text larger or smaller. But unfortunately, any jpgs in the book will pretty much remain the same size that they were in the original word doc. This can make the Kindle book look pretty bad and also make it difficult to really see the pictures. So, I usually create a separate Word Doc for the Kindle file and change the paper size in it to 8 ½ x 11. Then, I adjust the jpg pictures accordingly so that they are as large as possible. Tip: In Kindle, you can zoom pictures by using ctrl+ to zoom.

Another consideration for the Word Doc files (for both the printed book and the ebook) is hyperlinks. If you have written a "how-to" book, it may contain many hyperlinks. Remember to remove the underlines for all the hyperlinked text for the paperback book file. If you don't remove them, people trying to type a website address into their browser from your printed book may not notice that the address contains some underscores. It will be more annoying for them to have to retype the web address than to get it right the first time.

 However, in the Kindle book, it is fine to keep the underlines on the hyperlinks because they may simply click on them to get to their desired website destination. That's a really valuable reason for uploading a Word Doc to be converted to Kindle. Sadly, when converting PDF files to Kindle, all hyperlinking is lost in the conversion process.

Process For Producing Fully Illustrated Books

 I do not use a CreateSpace interior template for illustrated children's books. I do not like to use Microsoft Word for children's picture books because it is virtually impossible to format Word so that the pictures extend to the edge of the paper. I personally use Microsoft Publisher but there are many other graphics programs available. Any program used for creating newsletters can be used for formatting illustrated books.

If you want your picture to cover the entire book page, remember that the background colors and image may extend completely to the paper edges but any text or important graphic images must be contained in an area at least 1/2" inside the entire border of the printed paper size. Otherwise, you risk having it cut off in the printing process. Or worse, if an image extends across 2 pages, you might lose any important imagery in the center of the book. Just keep those things in mind as you're designing the image.

Sample Illustrated Double Page Spread from Sandi Johnson's – "Book 6 – Dorp The Scottish Dragon in a Lone Star Story"

Everyone was so excited about the babies they didn't notice Britt peering around a corner muttering to herself, "That's just great. More dragons to mess with!" She left the barn to the dragons.

Dorp beamed as Yonga held their youngsters out to him. "Yehaw! The Texas Twins", he cried. "We'll name them Haley and Ally."

All of a sudden there was a loud screeching and wailing. Dorp turned excitedly to see his friends from Scotland had arrived for the big party. They were marching into the barn playing their bagpipes and drums.

"Time to celebrate, my friends! Let's all go outside for the feast," Dorp invited all to join the family for a picnic in the yard.

A special note about jpgs: If you have produced your own illustrations by hand, you will need to scan them to 300 DPI jpg files so that you can insert them into your electronic book file. If you are using photographs, try to only use photos taken with a digital camera. The picture files will automatically be saved to jpg format when the picture is taken. You can just insert those into the program you are using to create your book. You can use scans of printed photographs (especially pictures to be used in a family recollections book) but the quality is not going to be as sharp and clear as a photo from a digital camera.

START PRODUCING BOOK FILES AND JPGS

Through this process you will be working with the following Microsoft Publisher (or other graphics program) files:

1. Master-Book Title.pub – This file will contain everything to create the book (text boxes and jpgs). You will do all creating and all editing in this file.

2. All JPGs-Book Title.pub – This file will contain jpgs only. No text boxes! It will contain all parts of the book. – You will upload the small size PDF you create from it to KDP Select for the Kindle ebook file.

3. Interior Only – Book Title.pub – This file will contain jpgs only. No text boxes! It will not contain the front or back book cover or the blank inside covers. – You will upload the large size PDF you create from it to CreateSpace for your printed book.

4. Book Cover File.pub – This file will contain both the front and back book covers on one "page" – back of book on the left side and front of the book on the right side. You will upload the large size PDF you create from it to CreateSpace for the printed book.

I start an illustrated book project with one Microsoft Publisher file containing all of the book pages (including front and back cover and blank inside front and back covers). Each page will contain all of the separate data (jpgs of illustrations, content text, page numbers, etc.). Name this Microsoft Publisher file "Master-Book Title". In fact, it is best to use abbreviations for the title, ie...book title "123 - Count With Me" becomes "123-CWM".

Once a page in the "Master-Book Title" (*Master-123-CWM*) file has been laid out exactly as it should be, save that page to the highest quality jpg - at least 300 dpi. Name the jpg of that page with a description which will distinguish it. For fully illustrated books, only number the actual story pages 1, 2, 3, 4, 5, etc. This will place them in the correct book order in a directory folder.

All other pages should be as follows: Title Page should be named Title Page. Cover Page should be named Cover Page. All optional pages should have a name describing their purpose such as Song Lyrics, Author Page, etc. This makes it much easier to find pages that need to be edited later.

Create a folder in which to place all of the individual JPGS. Place all of the finished jpgs there. Folder structure and file naming conventions are extremely important to the entire book producing process. You wouldn't believe how many files you end up with by the end of book production. Unless you're filing things properly, you could very easily lose or misplace vital parts and pieces of information or worse, use the wrong or outdated file.

Once every page in the book has been laid out perfectly and all of the jpgs have been created, save the "Master-Book Title" (*Master-123-CWM*) file and then create a copy of it.

The 2nd Microsoft Publisher file should be named "All JPGs-Book Title" (*All JPGS-123-CWM*). Replace all data on each page of that file with the proper jpg for each individual page. This includes front and back covers, title page, copyright|isbn|bisac page, book content and all other pages of the book. Do not get rid of the blank pages. Save this file and create a copy of it.

Name the 3rd copy of the Microsoft Publisher file "Interior Only – Book Title" (*Interior Only-123-CWM*). Remove the front and back book cover and the blank pages. Save the file.

Convert or save the 3rd Microsoft Publisher "Interior Only – Book Title" (*Interior Only-123-CWM*) file to the highest quality PDF possible. Keep the same name for the pdf as for the Microsoft Publisher file.

The directory structure and content will look similar to this

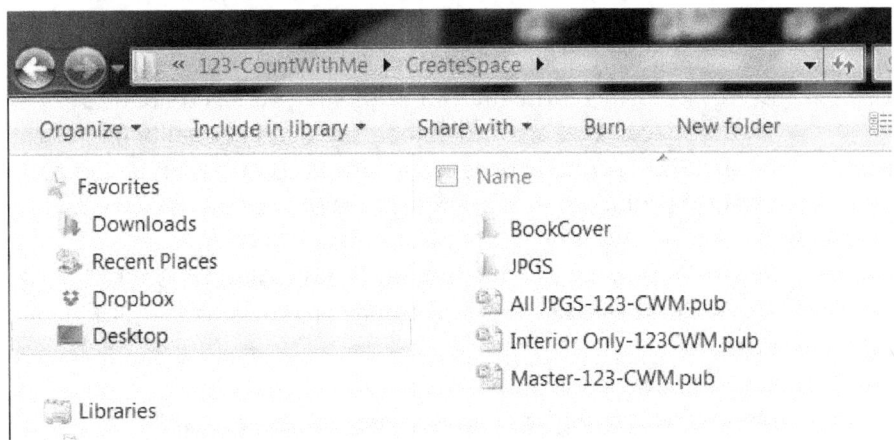

Open the #3 "Interior Only – Book Title" (*Interior Only-123-CWM*) PDF file to review for errors. If there are any errors, make any and all changes to the #1 Microsoft Publisher "Master-Book Title" (*Master-123-CWM*) file. In fact, ALWAYS perform all edits in the #1 Microsoft Publisher "Master-Book Title" (*Master-123-CWM*) file.

NOTE: *The only jpgs which should be in the #1 Microsoft Publisher "Master-Book Title" (Master-123-CWM) file are those containing artwork or illustrations only...no embedded text. Of course, if the artwork or illustration contains stylized text, purposely placed there by the artist, that is acceptable. All other data on these pages should be contained in actual text boxes.*

Create new jpgs for all pages which were edited. Insert them into both #2 Microsoft Publisher "All JPGs-Book Title" (*All JPGS-123-CWM*) and #3 Microsoft Publisher "Interior Only-Book Title" (*Interior Only-123-CWM*) files.

Create a new PDF file from the #3 Microsoft Publisher "Interior Only-Book Title" (*Interior Only-123-CWM*) file and check for errors again.

Do this as many times as necessary until everything is perfect.

The final #3 "Interior Only – Book Title" (*Interior Only-123-CWM*) PDF will be the Interior Book file you will upload to CreateSpace. You need to upload the highest quality file for the book to be printed in order to insure the sharpest quality and brightest colors on the printed pages of the soft cover book.

Open the final #2 Microsoft Publisher file All JPGs-Book Title (*All JPGS-123-CWM*) file. Save or convert to the smallest PDF file possible.

Note: *The reason for creating the AllJPGS-123CWM.pub file in the first place is because when you convert a PDF file containing a mixture of text and jpgs, the contents of the PDF file have a tendency to become somewhat jumbled up in the KDP conversion process. Conversions of pdfs containing all jpg files turn out much more organized and pleasing to the eye than conversions of pdf files containing mixed content.*

Note: *Most Microsoft Publisher files for illustrated books are very large so, if you can't do the file conversion to PDF yourself, save your Microsoft Publisher file to a jump drive and ask a friend or family member to do the conversion to pdf for you.*

The All JPGs-Book Title (*All JPGS-123-CWM*) small PDF file is the entire book file format which you will use to convert to Kindle through the Kindle Kid's Book Creator, which is available for Free (more on that program later). The reason for uploading a file containing the front and back book cover to Amazon is because the Kindle upload process deletes the front book cover. This will leave the Title page intact as the first page of the Kindle file.

The reason for uploading a very small pdf file is because large files take a very long time to download to a Kindle reader and that will annoy the heck out of potential readers. Large files

might not display properly on Kindle, either. Small files look just
as good and download very quickly. Do yourself and your
potential readers a favor and remember this step.

To summarize: Building your illustrated book will require
working with 3 separate Microsoft Publisher files. You will end
up with 2 final PDF files. One large PDF for uploading the
interior content to CreateSpace for the printed book and the
other is a small PDF for uploading the entire book file to Kindle.

NOTE: *If you do not have a program that does this, there are
FREE online programs which will convert the original file type
and then email a pdf file to you. Just do a search on Convert to
PDF and select the proper file type to convert from.*

When creating the PDF, take the books dimensions into
consideration. If the Microsoft Word document is set up to be
5" x 8" (such as for a romance novel), then the page size for the
PDF must also be set up for that size. The Adobe PDF settings
must also be set to Embed All Fonts. After the Adobe PDF
preferences have been set you may Create the PDF. If you have
Acrobat Pro, you may Convert to PDF, Save to PDF or Print to
PDF. Once the PDF is created, review the PDF file and correct
any errors. Microsoft Word 2007 and newer versions allow you
to SaveAs a PDF file.

The book cover will require a separate PDF file. Follow the
instructions in the "Produce The Book Cover" section of this
book.

NOTE: *Whatever you do, DO NOT use a printer to scan your
entire book to PDF. The quality will not be good enough.*

Produce the Book Cover

CreateSpace offers you the ability to create a book cover for
FREE through their site. Their online book cover program will
assist you in creating a nice design that can even include
pictures. There are many designs to choose from. It is worth it
to look into what they offer.

If you have Microsoft Publisher or another graphics program,
then it is best to create the book cover with that. One reason is
because the CreateSpace Book Cover Generator does not allow
you to save the cover image to your computer. You can capture
the image with a program like "Snipping Tool" or something like
that but the quality of the image might be grainy. I know
because I did exactly that for the covers of all four volumes of
my Phrase Thesaurus books. Since I had chosen to use the
CreateSpace Cover Generator for those books, I found myself in
quite a pickle when it came time to upload files to Lightening
Source for distributing my books through their network. *More
on Lightening Source later.*

NOTE: *A valuable lesson learned from that experience is that it
is best to create the covers yourself or have an artist do it in
order to maintain the highest quality of the images.*

You will need the book cover image in PDF format if you are
going to publish your book through any source other than
CreateSpace. Get a Lightening Source/Ingram Spark book cover
generated at
***https://myaccount.lightningsource.com/Portal/Tools/CoverTe
mplateGenerator*** . The book cover templates for different
companies are never laid out the same so you will have to redo
them every time you publish with someone else. Also, in
marketing efforts, you'll always need a jpg of the front book
cover to upload and share with different sources.

*This is an example of a book cover that I "snipped" from
the CreateSpace Cover Generator.*

If you are going to use Microsoft Publisher, download the proper CreateSpace Cover Template for your book size. Configure CreateSpace templates at

https://www.createspace.com/Help/Book/Artwork.do

Required information for generating a cover template will include Interior Type (Full Color, Black and White, etc), Trim Size (8"x10", 6"x9", etc), and number of pages (not counting front and back book covers or blank inside book covers). CreateSpace will send you a template with a .png extension. This extension will work the same as a .jpg file.

A CreateSpace book cover template includes both the space for both front and back of the book cover. The template includes everything you see in the following example. The back of the book cover is placed on the left side of the "page" and the front of the book cover is placed on the right side of the "page". Spine text is centered. There is a lot of extra space around the actual book cover. Each printing company sets up book templates to suit the requirements of their machinery.

Example of CreateSpace Cover Template for Help Yourself Book Cover

By the time you get around to creating this book cover, you should have already completed the separate front and back covers to be included in the #1 Microsoft Publisher "Master-Book Title" (*Master-123-CWM*) file and created 300 DPI jpgs for each of them. Use those JPGS (for the front and back book covers) for inserting into the combined front/back Book Cover file.

The CreateSpace book cover template will show the exact dimensions that your Microsoft Publisher Book Cover file should be set up for. For Instance: If you want your final book to be printed at 6" x 9" and there will be 44 pages in the book, set up the Microsoft Publisher Book Cover page size to 19" X 13". The trim edge of this particular book will be 12.1" x 9". If you change the number of pages, the trim edge dimension will change, so you must generate a new template, in that case.

Insert the CreateSpace .png template into the Microsoft
Publisher page and expand the template to completely cover
the edges of the blank Microsoft Publisher page. In the 6x9
Book Cover Example, you will see several guide lines drawn on
the template. The outer lines show where the edges of your
front and back cover jpgs should be when you insert them. The
inner set of lines shows wherein the text and any important
graphics should be contained.

Here is an example of a 6" x 9" book cover - This is how it
looks in Microsoft Publisher with the CreateSpace template
behind it and the additional guidelines on top.

Note that you cannot actually see the images on the
CreateSpace template as they are completely covered by the
artwork.

Also note that the white space is the 19" wide by 13" high
CreateSpace template. The back of this book cover contains the
space for the Bar Code.

If your jpgs have been properly formatted, you will not need to worry about the inner lines. The two sets of dashed lines in the middle of the template show the width of the book spine. If a spine is less than 1/2" wide, no text is allowed on the spine. This would work out to about 150 pages. If you place text there anyway, CreateSpace will remove it. TIP: I usually draw lines over those lines and extend them beyond the borders of the page so that I can easily see them. It helps to keep all elements of the book cover where they belong. Don't forget to erase any lines you drew before creating a PDF file for the book cover.

I always place a rectangle shape behind the book cover jpgs so that my book cover does not have to have a white spine. I color the rectangle to match the colors of the jpgs.

Once everything is properly placed in the Microsoft Publisher Book Cover file, delete the CreateSpace template from the page. Save or convert the Microsoft Publisher Book Cover file as a high quality PDF. Open the PDF to review. If there are any errors, open the Microsoft Publisher file and fix them. Create another PDF. If everything is good, this is the PDF file you will upload to CreateSpace for the book cover.

Notes about the book cover files:

Front Book Cover

The front book cover needs to be as visually appealing as possible. It should include Book Title, Subtitle (if any), Author name and Illustrator name (if any). Graphics or pictures are great but not essential to all books but most should have some kind of picture indicating the content of the book. No other information is required on the front book cover.

Note: *If you are creating your own book cover and are interested in purchasing images for it or even for the interior of your book, try Dreamstime.com. Sometimes, they offer images*

*for free. I have purchased images from them for as little as
$1.00 each. Just keep your searches confined to "Level 0" for
that price. Purchasing these images gives you the right to use
them for any of your projects – books, websites and other
marketing purposes.*

Back Book Cover

A lot of information is important for the back of a book. This is
where a short but concise book description should go. I call this
the "Sell Text" but it is more commonly called the "Sales Copy".
Sometimes you might hear it referred to as the "Promotional
Text". Potential readers may or may not decide to read or
purchase a book depending on this text. Give it a lot of thought
and do the best job you can when writing it.

When you design the back of a book cover you must leave space
at the top left corner for the BISAC codes and space at the
bottom right corner for the ISBN number. You will be
responsible for listing the BISAC Codes yourself. CreateSpace
will print the ISBN number on the back cover at the time a Print
On Demand (POD) book is ordered by a customer. So, all you
need to do is leave the proper amount of space for the ISBN
number. That would be about 2 ½" wide by 1 ¼" high. It may
vary depending on the actual size of the book.

Another element for most back book covers is graphics. Some
people choose to put a picture of the author on the back cover
and others choose to use a picture that indicates the content of
the book. That is entirely personal preference. My preference
in children's books is to use a partial illustration from the
interior of the book.

Upload files to CreateSpace

All of the book production is complete and approved by you and your editor. Now, you're finally ready to publish that book! Whoo-hoo! What a relief...you have produced all of the necessary files without spending anything on them but your time.

These next steps are absolutely FREE, also. CreateSpace charges nothing at all for you to upload your files. You may review (or proof) them and approve them as many times as necessary before publishing.   So, here's what you need to do next.

Upload Formatted Book

Login to your CreateSpace account and access your book project. Click on the tab to upload your interior file. By now, your book size should have already been nailed down, so select the size you previously decided upon. You will also select the paper color. Books containing color illustrations are only available to be printed on white paper. Anything else may be printed on crème colored paper. Select whether you want the book images to extend beyond the paper edges or not. For books containing text only, you would not want the text to extend beyond the paper.

For illustrated books, you will choose based on how you set up your interior pages. It is not always possible to set up illustrated books so that the images extend to the edges of the page. For instance, you might be using older images which were formatted for a different page size or not formatted so that all important stylized text or images fit within a 1/2" border all around the page. In that case, you will have to select "image does not extend to edge of page".

Browse your computer to select your interior file. Once it is
uploaded, you will then be allowed to either create your cover
using CreateSpace's online program or upload the cover file that
you have prepared.

If you are using CreateSpace's online cover creator, just follow
all of the instructions as you go along. You will be able to make
as many changes to the cover as needed so keep working with it
until you are happy with the final result. If you are using the
cover you created outside of CreateSpace, browse to it on your
computer and upload.

Within a few minutes after your interior file upload is complete,
you will have the opportunity to look at an electronic version of
your book. Review the book very carefully.

If you see any errors, reject the book, make the changes to your
Microsoft Word or Publisher Document and go through the
upload process again.

You may see some symbols on the electronic book review that
worry you. For instance, a symbol might indicate that the image
is not 300 dpi. If you know you saved your jpgs to 300 dpi, then
don't worry about that error symbol. Sometimes, it occurs
when you have created a jpg from all text. This usually does not
create a problem with the actual visual images in the ebook or
the printed book. You must realize, though, that if you started
out with a blurred image, you are going to see a blurred image
on both the ebook and printed book. Make sure you are only
working with files that have sharp clear lines.

Another error might suggest that the image is over the confines
of the border of the page. Once again, this can be a false error.
Visually judge for yourself when doing the electronic review.
You will be able to tell if this is really going to be a problem or
not when the book is printed.

If you decide to make any changes after this electronic review of the interior file, remember, for fully illustrated books, to make them on the #1 Microsoft Publisher Master-Book Title (Master-123-CWM) file and fix the #2 (All JPG-123-CWM) and #3(Interior Only-123-CWM) files from that. You can repeat this process as many times as necessary to perfect your files.

Note: *Change the file name each time you re-upload to CreateSpace to avoid any potential confusion. Simply adding -1, -2, -3 to the new file is a good enough difference in filename.*

When you are finally happy with everything on the electronic review, approve the interior file.

Once the electronic interior file is approved by you, you will be allowed to submit it to CreateSpace for review by a real person at that company. This review process usually takes 24 or more hours.

If the book passes this review, you will be given another opportunity for an electronic book review. You will see the book cover and the book interior in this review. Take as much time as required to thoroughly check for errors. You still have the opportunity to make corrections, if you find anything wrong. If everything is just as you desire, you can approve the book right then and there and the soft cover print version of your book will be made available for sale to the public immediately.

STOP!

ORDER A PHYSICAL PROOF

I wouldn't be so quick to give final approval, based on the electronic review alone. In my opinion, you really need a physical proof – a real printed copy of your book - in your hands before you can possibly really know how it is going to look in print. So, although everything has been FREE up to this point, I highly recommend that you order a physical proof before giving final approval to make the book available to the public for sale. **But you absolutely do not have to if you don't want to.**

If you do want to order a printed proof, immediately after you exit the electronic review screen, simply click on the "Order A Printed Proof" link. No matter what type of book you are publishing, one printed proof should cost much less than $10.00 total including shipping and handling. Text-only books will just cost a couple of dollars. It is money well spent. And you can order up to 4 physical proofs if you want to at this time. This is always a good idea, especially if you are working with a co-writer or illustrator or if you'd like for your editor or beta readers to have a physical copy to edit. It will take a week or so for the book(s) to arrive so be patient. I know that will be very hard. I've been there many times.

SET UP PRICING AND DISTRIBUTION

In the meantime, if you haven't already done so, you can begin setting up the distribution and pricing for your book. From the Homepage for your Book Project in CreateSpace, click on Channels, under the Distribute section. Here you can determine where you want your book to be distributed. Remember, as I mentioned earlier, you must have a BISAC code in order for your book to be distributed to certified resellers such as independent bookstores and book resellers that CreateSpace is associated with. The CreateSpace Direct program allows eligible resellers to buy books at wholesale prices directly from

CreateSpace. Most of these resellers are going to be other
online book stores, not brick and mortar stores.

Once you've completed the Distribution Channels section, go to
the Pricing section. CreateSpace will determine and show you
the minimum price that your book may be sold for. This will be
based on how many pages are in the book, color or type of
paper, whether or not you have color pictures and other things.

You can price your book at any price you wish over the
suggested retail price. Just don't get too greedy because you do
want your book to "sell", don't you? Two or 3 dollars over the
suggested price is reasonable.   You'll also see suggested prices
for Amazon partners in Europe and other places around the
world. And you'll see your potential royalties per each sale.

SET UP BOOK DISCRIPTION AND KEY WORDS

Click the Description Link on the left side of your book project
page in CreateSpace to enter a description for the book, the
BISAC category, Author Biography, Book Language, Search
Keywords and some other information. The description should
match what you have on the back of the book but you can
expand upon that here. This description will be duplicated on
the Amazon page for your book also.

The BISAC categories should match that inside the book and on
the back cover.

The Author Biography is optional but it is highly recommended
and something you may want to link to from many different
social media sites.

Search Keywords are super important. They are a vital part of
the metadata for your book that allows potential customers to
find your book via search engines. Keywords absolutely must
be related to the content of your book. Go to Amazon and do

some searches on books that are similar to yours. What keywords did you use to find those books? See what words or phrases they used in their book descriptions. Are you using similar terminology? Remember, keywords may be single words or phrases.

Google also has a keyword search tool that you can use to look up the most popular terms for your subject matter. Of course, you will have to have a Google Adwords account to access it.

Learn more about it here.
https://support.google.com/adwords/answer/2999770?hl=en

YOUR BOOK AVAILABLE FOR SALE ONLINE

Once your book is available for purchase on Amazon websites, it will also be available for potential customers to *request* in brick and mortar stores. If a customer asks for your book, the store will look it up in their database and discover that it is available as a Print On Demand (POD) book. They will order it for the customer and the customer will be able to pick it up at the store in a couple of weeks. If enough customers did this, it's possible that the store might possibly stock the book.

It is not highly likely, though because CreateSpace does not allow brick and mortar stores to return unsold books. This practice discourages stores from purchasing books wholesale from them. In order to entice physical stores to purchase your printed books for their book shelves, you will need to go the extra mile of publishing it through a company like Lightning Source or Ingram Spark. This is not free, but they will allow for unsold book returns. More on that later.

Publish The Book

PUBLISH (Print Book) THROUGH CREATESPACE

If you waited to review the physical printed proof before
publishing, you have been wise. Even after all of your hard
work and eagle eye checking, it's still possible the book will
require changes. If so, then just go back through all the
previous steps and re-submit the book through CreateSpace. If
the book is exactly as you've hope it would be, then you will log
back into CreateSpace to approve the printed book to be made
available for sale through Amazon and all of CreateSpace's
other online book selling partners.

NOTE: *This will not automatically create a Kindle ebook!*

PUBLISH (Ebook) ON KDP Select

*Note: I think, in the not too distant past, Kindle changed its
conversion process because I've noticed lately, that most of the
time, when using a PDF file to convert to Kindle, the conversion
process drops pages from the Kindle ebook. Amazon obviously
became aware of this at some point and decided to offer a
program to remedy this. It is called the "Kindle Kids' Book
Creator". This program is very simple to use and I believe it has
become absolutely essential that you do use it to create your
Kindle .mobi file. Get the Kindle Kid's Book Creator at
https://kdp.amazon.com/how-to-publish-childrens-books*

*Once you've installed it, simply import the small pdf file you've
already created, containing the book cover and all of the other
pictures in the book. It will create a perfect .mobi file which you
may upload to KDP.*

You will need to set up an account with KDP Select to publish
the Kindle ebook. ***Do that at https://kdp.amazon.com/***

If you have a KDP account, once you have approved your printed book, you may publish it on Kindle directly from CreateSpace. Simply click the button that says "Publish My Book On Kindle". That will take you to your KDP Select account where, on the left hand side of the screen, you will see the book cover for your new book.

You will also see the ASIN number for the Kindle book. If you want that number to appear on the printed or ebooks, you could, at this time, redo all of your files to include that number. Personally, I don't feel it's all that important so I don't do those extra steps. This is something for you to make up your own mind about.

Work through all of the KDP Select sections until you've set up your book the way you want. When you get to the section that asks whether you want KDP Select to convert your file from CreateSpace or if you want to upload another file, select, Upload Another File. Browse your computer to the #2 Small All Jpgs.pdf file which you created or use the .mobi file that you created using Kindle Kid's Book Creator. Remember, both are small size files which are easy to down load. Either file should also contain the Front and Back cover of the book. I have found that KDP Select always removes the front cover of Kindle books. I find that pretty annoying and don't really understand the reasoning for it. It also makes for a very important reason to have a Title Page with an image of the book cover on it.

Once the file finishes uploading, you will have the opportunity to preview the ebook. Make sure you do that because you never really know if everything is perfect. If everything looks as it should, then approve the file and you are done!

It usually takes 24 hours or so for a Kindle book to appear on Amazon. If at any time, you want to make your Kindle ebook free, simply log back into KDP select and make that selection.

You may find that to be a great way to market your book. Lots of sites will list Kindle books that are free.

You may wonder why you'd want to give your book away. One reason is exposure. People love free stuff. Also, especially for books with illustrations, seeing the entire ebook may inspire purchases of the printed books. Once again, offering your Kindle book for free is purely optional.

You may also offer your Kindle ebook for free when you enroll it in Matchbook. It is a program that allows Amazon customers who purchased your physical books to be given a discount on the e-book version of the same title. The price range choices you have are from $2.99 to free. Customers who have purchased your printed book are only offered the option of a free to $2.99 ebook if you, the author, has chosen to take part in the program.

Note: As of February 2017, KDP began offering print books through windows that popped up immediately after your kindle book was processed. This has caused a great deal of confusion and frustration amongst authors since most independent authors have been using CreateSpace for print books sold through Amazon.

There have been many pro and con articles written on whether or not it's worth it to switch from CreateSpace to KDP Print. Before you make any decisions on the subject you need to know that you cannot just switch back and forth between the two without causing yourself a lot of trouble. Here are a couple of the better comparison articles to help you make your decision on which is better for your needs.

https://kindlepreneur.com/createspace-vs-kdp-print/

https://wordwave.pub/kdp-print-vs-createspace-which-is-better/

As a matter of fact, I'm leaning more toward this author's
perspective. **https://dianetibert.com/2017/04/17/amazons-
new-kdp-print-feature-is-bad-news-for-createspace-users/**

Google Play Books – Before I go much further, I wanted to let
you know Google Play Books is another free source for making
your ebook available to the public for sale.

Go here to check it out -
https://play.google.com/books/publish/ .

You will need a Gmail account in order to sign up for it. The
reason I'm mentioning this now is because you may upload PDF
files to Google Play Books and you will happen to have a PDF file
by this point.

You may also upload epub files there. You don't have to worry
about providing your own ISBN number with Google Play Books
either. If you don't have one, they will assign one for the book.
Your files will be DRM (Digital Rights Management) protected
and you can determine how much of the book people may read
for free before they decide to purchase it. No one will be able
to print, cut, copy, or save anything from the preview pages
displaying book content. The good news is that your book on
Google Play will be available in a Google search. As with
CreateSpace, you will have to provide bank account information
in order to be paid.

NOTE: *I must warn you, the Google Play interface is not user
friendly at all. It might take a lot of time and effort to finally get
your books registered there.*

Promote Your Book

SET UP YOUR FREE AMAZON ASSOCIATE ACCOUNT

Amazon offers the opportunity for anyone with a blog or website to make money off of any products that anyone sells through Amazon. Once you begin marketing your book through your own blog or website, you will want to take advantage of those opportunities to list your own books for sale there with your own Amazon Associate codes. You will actually make a little more money off the sale of each of your books that get sold that way.

You may also decide to try listing other author's books for sale on your blog or website, too. Plus, potential book reviewers who have their own blogs or websites might be more encouraged to review your book if they know they can link to it on Amazon through their own associate account. Everyone wins when a book gets sold from a "click" through an associate link. Go to *https://affiliate-program.amazon.com/* to join.

Once again, you will need a bank account number to join so that you may be paid.   You may use your social security number as your tax id.

Note: *Regarding payments to you – As your books begin to sell, you will begin receiving royalty payments from CreateSpace, Amazon and KDP Select within 3 months of the first purchases of your books. These payments (if any) will be automatically deposited into your bank account every month after that. Royalties vary for every type of book and service.*

Promote and Market Your Book For FREE

There are very many places to publicize your book for FREE. But
in this case, I have to say the word FREE is relative. I don't know
about you but my time is very valuable to me. So, every minute
that I spend trying to promote a book is precious time taken
away from my other writings. Regardless, I'd rather spend as
few actual dollars in promotional endeavors as possible as I'm
sure you must feel the same. Below you will learn about many
ways to promote your book without spending a penny to do so.
Some of the best sources are Facebook, Pinterest, Youtube and
GoodReads. And remember, each of those social media sites
have many variations on the theme so do some research on
other competitors options. Get creative in your searches.

Claim Your Amazon Author Central Page

Before we get into those other sites mentioned above, I want to
tell you about the value of claiming your Amazon Author Central
page. When you look up a book on Amazon, you will notice that
the author's name is listed between the book title and the book
description. You will see that their name is underlined. That
means that there is a link to the Author's Page on Amazon.
Many potential buyers click this link in order to learn about the
author and to see what other books they might have available.
Amazon provides that information for all books of all authors
but you must "claim" your author page in order to be able to
edit the information on it. Your author page on Amazon is very
valuable real estate. It is the place where you will have an
opportunity to list your author bio, all of your books, your blog
or website, pictures, book trailers and more. You can access
mine at this link to see what they look like.
https://www.amazon.com/-/e/B009K3WGMS The page the
public sees looks like this:

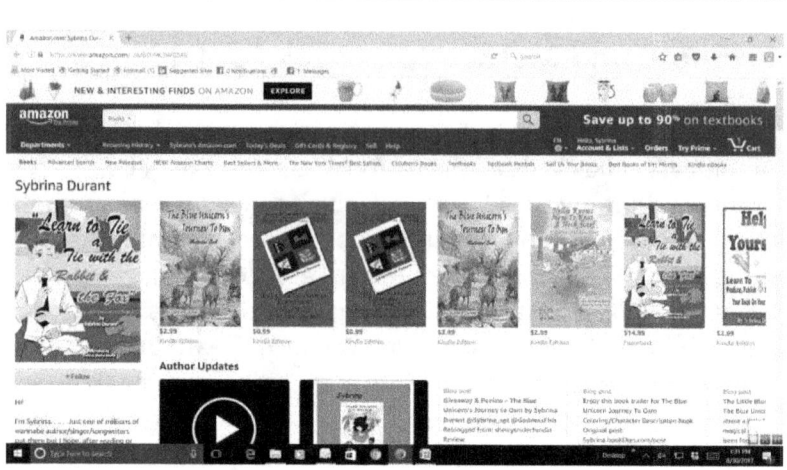

It's a good idea to include your Amazon Author page link in your email signature or on Twitter, Facebook and other places. You can even link it from your Goodreads author page.

When you are logged into your Author Central site it will look like what you see below.

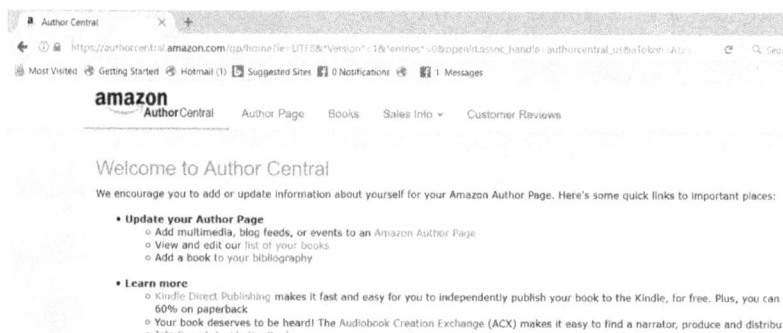

Click the Author Page tab to start adding everything you want people to know about you.

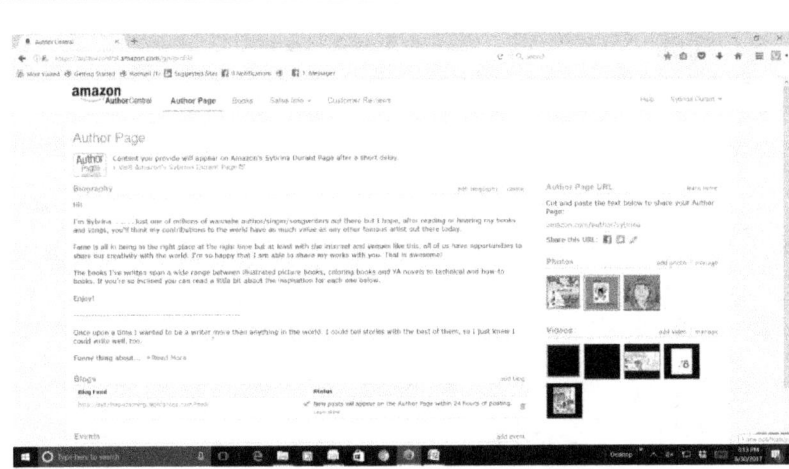

Click the Book Tab to "claim" your books. Here's what mine looks like.

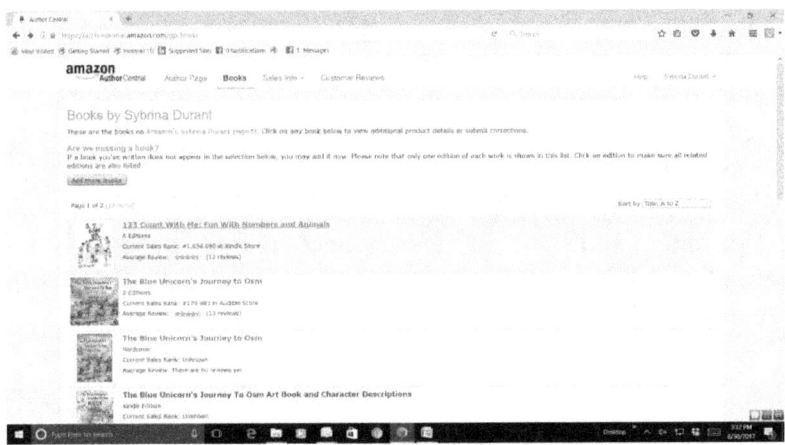

After you add your books, you can also add Editorial Reviews for them. You might be wondering why you would need to do that. It turns out that many review services, especially the most noted (and super expensive) ones like Kirkus, Publisher's Weekly, or Library Journal will not post a review on your book page because they don't want to get sideways with Amazon. So, Amazon has kindly provided a place where authors may

feature these very important reviews. You may add several for
each book.

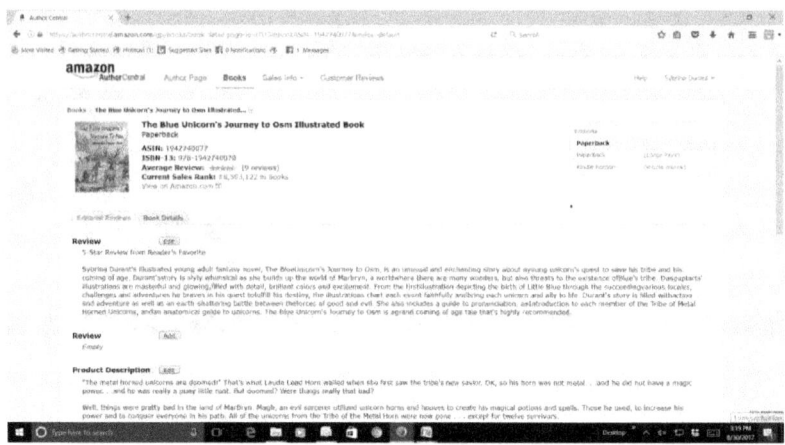

 In addition to Author and Book pages there are a few other
cool things you might want to know about. Click the Sales Info
tab. From it, you can actually see your Neilsen BookScan Rank
(point of sale data for book sales), your Sales Rank (among all
books sold on Amazon in your category) and your Author Rank
(among all Amazon Authors). All of this is pretty cool
information and some authors can become quite obsessed
about it. Here's my Author Ranking for one of my books back in
August 2017.

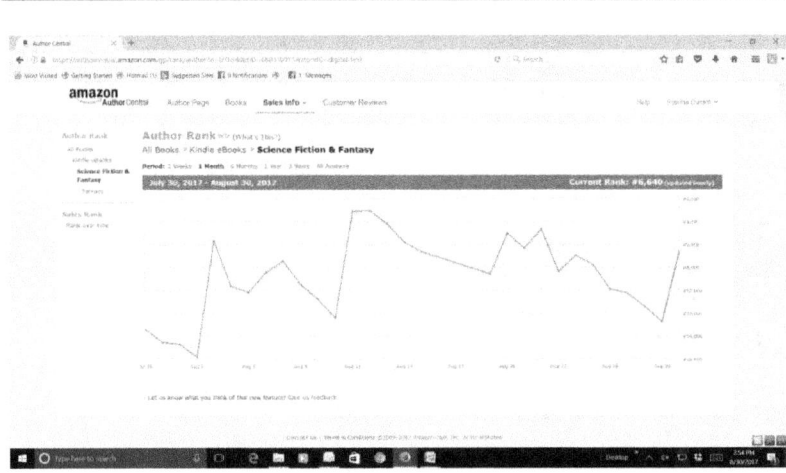

There is also a Review Tab where you can see all of your
Amazon Customer Reviews in one place.

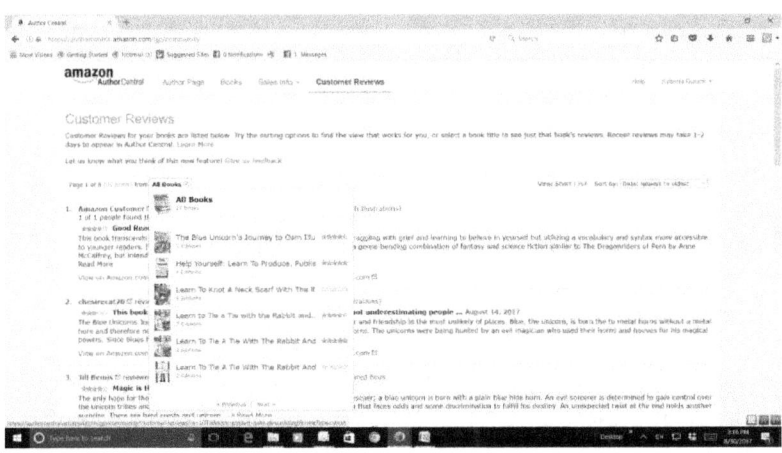

You can sort by book and from lowest or highest ranking. This
tool saves you a lot of time searching for reviews on your book
sales pages on Amazon…especially if you have a lot of books.

By the way, all countries have Amazon Author pages but they
don't always look the same. You must realize that when you log
on to *Amazon.com*, you are logging on to Amazon in the United
States. Amazon sites in other countries have their own web

addresses. As such, if your Author Page is on the American site, it is only seen by the people who login to the American site. This makes it important for you to also claim and populate your Author pages for other countries.

The web address for Amazon in the United States is *https://www.amazon.com*.

https://www.amazon.co.uk is for United Kingdom

https://www.amazon.ca is for Canada

https://www.amazon.com.au is for Australia

https://www.amazon.fr is for France and Monaco

https://www.amazon.de is for Germany, Austria, Luxembourg, Switzerland, and Liechtenstein

https://www.amazon.it is for Italy, San Marino, Vatican City and Switzerland

https://www.amazon.com.mx is for Mexico

https://www.amazon.br is for Brazil

https://www.amazon.es is for Spain, including Canary Islands, Balearic Islands, Ceuta, and Melilla

https://www.amazon.co.jp is for Japan

https://www.amazon.in is for India

Once your book is published through Createspace or Kindle you can go to those websites above and look up your books.

Not all foreign Amazon sites have Author Central pages that can be edited, though. The web addresses for the ones that do are

https://authorcentral.amazon.com for US

https://authorcentral.amazon.co.uk for United Kingdom

https://authorcentral.amazon.fr for France

https://authorcentral.amazon.de for Germany

and

https://authorcentral.amazon.co.jp for Japan.

Right now you may be thinking...What???? I can't speak any language other than English! How the heck am I going to know what is on those pages. Not to worry...there are many online translators available for your use absolutely free these days. If you use the Chrome web browser, just utilize the quick translate button for foreign sites.

Most of these Author Central sites (except for Japan) allow you to log in with the same user name and password as your home country. You will have to register separately for Japan. Once you get logged in and claim your Author Page on a foreign site, make sure that you try to include everything from your home site.

After you have completed adding everything to your author pages, you will be given a new web address that you can share with others like this one: *https://www.amazon.com/-/e/B009K3WGMS*

Learn To Work Facebook

If you don't already have one, create a Facebook page for your author marketing activities. Name the account Your Name – Author. This can be an extension of your existing account or if you want to write anonymously, then set up a new account using a different email address. Set the page up so that people can LIKE it.

Learn about setting up Facebook product pages here.
https://www.facebook.com/business/goals/launch-new-product#set-up-your-page

Of course, Facebook is going to encourage you to purchase advertising for your product page but you do not have to.

Visit my Facebook Product Page here.
https://www.facebook.com/SybrinaPublishing

I would really appreciate a "Like" from you while you're there. Other Facebook Product pages that I've created are

https://www.facebook.com/pages/Learn-To-Tie-With-The-Rabbit-And-The-Fox/798807016841129 and

https://www.facebook.com/pages/Sybrinas-Phrase-Thesaurus/455360197949377 and

https://www.facebook.com/The-Blue-Unicorns-Journey-To-Osm-794155627353303/ - Note about Product, Author or Book pages: These Facebook pages are set up with Review Tabs (or Links) for visitors to leave reviews of your product, service or even of you, yourself! Ask people who have provided reviews for your book elsewhere to also post their review of your book there.

Visit and Like my Facebook Author Page here.
https://www.facebook.com/SybrinaDurantChildrensBooksAut

hor   And if you message me to let me know you did so, I'll
return the favor and like your new page once you've created it.

Visit and Like the book store for my sister's Regency Romance
Novels - *https://www.facebook.com/ALittleBitOfRomance*

If you visited those four Facebook pages you should have seen a
"Shop Now" button next to the "Like" button. That button
takes you to my book publishing website but you can link it to
any web address that is most appropriate for your purposes,
including your book page on Amazon or CreateSpace. Make
sure you set up a "Shop Now" button on your author and/or
book page.

Also, read this article to learn how to create a Facebook Author
page. *http://www.standoutbooks.com/professional-author-
facebook-page/*

Facebook allows you to create many different types of pages.
You can create a business page, a company page, an author
page, a product (or book) page and many others. The more
ways you give people to find you the better.

The easiest way to market your book for FREE is to research and
join as many Facebook groups as you can to post your book
information to. Do this from your main Facebook page and post
links to your other Author or Product pages.

Posting on Facebook groups related to your book is the best
way to get FREE advertising. Don't limit yourself to joining book
or author groups. Do keyword searches to find groups that
might appreciate what you have to offer. If you write children's
books, join Mom Groups. Or join local swap and sell groups. Or
online craft show groups. If you write historical romances, find
groups about period dress and other things. Be creative in your
searches.

Once you have been approved as a member, READ THE GROUP
RULES! Most groups have files for member information. Lots
of times, the rules are listed at the top of the group's main
page. If not, then try clicking the files tab at the top of the
group page to find and read rules. Keep notes on each group.
Do they only allow business postings on certain days? If so,
then DO NOT post on any other days. And never post to a
group more than once a month or at the very most, once a
week. Anything more than that might be considered SPAM and
you don't want people to get that opinion of you. Try to keep
your postings fresh. Re-write your message constantly with
new twists and takes on your subject. (Cause if you post the
same exact words over and over, Facebook's algorithm will ding
you causing less people will see your posts.)

Create a spreadsheet so that you can keep track of group names
and rules on one tab. Create another tab to keep track of the
content of your posts for each group and the dates you last
posted. This will help insure that you don't come across as a
spammer.

Many Facebook Groups have "Like Ladders". This is a great way
to build up a fan base. Anyone who likes one of your pages will
then see your future posts on their newsfeed. You might just
develop some real fans that way and actually sell more of your
books. When you get involved in "Like Ladders", make sure you
have pasted the link from your Facebook page that you wish to
receive a "like" back for into the comment section of the like
ladder.

Since I have so many Facebook pages, I keep a notepad
document on my desktop with the web addresses for each of
them. That way, I can easily copy and paste the one I want for
the "Like Ladder" I'm working at the moment. The most
important rule about Like Ladders is to "Like" every single
Facebook product page on the list before you post the link to
your product page in the comment section.

Of course, if some page is offensive to you, you certainly do not have to "Like" that one. There are a few that I have not "Liked" because I just didn't want to see their offerings on my newsfeed. Also, you will be notified every time a Like Ladder is updated with new people and product pages. Try to always follow up with new people who join the "Like Ladder" after you. It can pay off in a big way.

I alternate listing different pages on Like Ladders. For children's and teen's book Like Ladders, I'll list ***https://www.facebook.com/pages/Learn-To-Tie-With-The-Rabbit-And-The-Fox/798807016841129*** or ***https://www.facebook.com/The-Blue-Unicorns-Journey-To-Osm-794155627353303/.*** For other reader groups, I'll list ***https://www.facebook.com/ALittleBitOfRomance*** and so on.

You can also use your Facebook page as a blog of sorts. Always provide a link to your book on Amazon, reviews of your book and/or your book trailer on each post. Share information revolving around the subject of your book. Share posts from similar sites.

They even have a "Notes" section where you can post articles you've written. Here's mine for The Blue Unicorn - ***https://www.facebook.com/pg/The-Blue-Unicorns-Journey-To-Osm-794155627353303/notes/?ref=page_internal*** . The best part about Facebook Notes is that Google will index them so others may find them. Here's a great article on the subject. ***https://www.socialmediaexaminer.com/use-facebook-notes-for-marketing/***

Make your Facebook page an informative place for people to land and "Like" or "Follow". All of that is FREE but for very small fees, you can boost your posts to everyone in your sphere of influence. That means to people in groups you belong to and to your friends. You may also post actual advertisements to the

general population on Facebook but that can start costing quite
a bit of money.

Note: *Facebook has a strange rule that an ad may not contain
more than 15% text. Many book covers have more text than
that so it's best to only use the book cover with no text or an
image with very little text. It's tempting to start spending
money but try to stick with the FREE stuff.*

GoodReads

GoodReads is the largest book reading website on the internet
with fifty five million registered readers as of the start of 2015.
In fact, the membership has been growing exponentially the
past few years. In 2012, there were 10,000,000 members. In
2013 there were 35,000,000. People are ravenously reading
books on this site.   It is affiliated with Amazon so there is a lot
of cross promotion going on between the two websites. There
are reading groups for every genre in existence on GoodReads.

You can join as many as you like. As a member you can join in
discussions about every subject under the sun. From time to
time, you'll find opportunities to give a little shout out to other
members about your book but most of the time, your input into
group discussions should not be self-serving. Try to stick to the
topics of discussion and develop some real relationships with
people in the groups. Author members should post all of their
books on their GoodReads author pages. All of the books will
have links for purchase. You will have the opportunity to
upload an entire book or a portion of a book, whichever you
prefer for previews.

Giving GoodReads members the opportunity to read a portion
of your book for FREE might encourage them to purchase it in
order to read the rest of the story. GoodReads is also a good
forum to find potential reviewers for your book.

Check out my GoodReads – Author Page here…
*https://www.goodreads.com/author/show/6455676.Sybrina_
Durant*.

All the features you see on that page are provided FREE to
Authors with a presence on GoodReads.

Another great Free service on GoodReads is something called
Listopia. Listopia provides thousands of different lists in
thousands of categories on which to feature your book. There
are several reasons for wanting to see your book on different
lists. The most important are 1) Anyone who finds a list will find
your book and possibly click on its link to learn more and 2)
Books on lists which have been voted on by many people move
higher up in Goodreads search engines making them easier to
be found. You can add your own books to any list you wish and
you may even create new lists. The only real drawback is that
you cannot vote on your own book.

My book , "The Blue Unicorn's Journey To Osm Illustrated Book
For Teen" is on several fantasy and illustrated book lists. You
can find them when you scroll down on the book page.

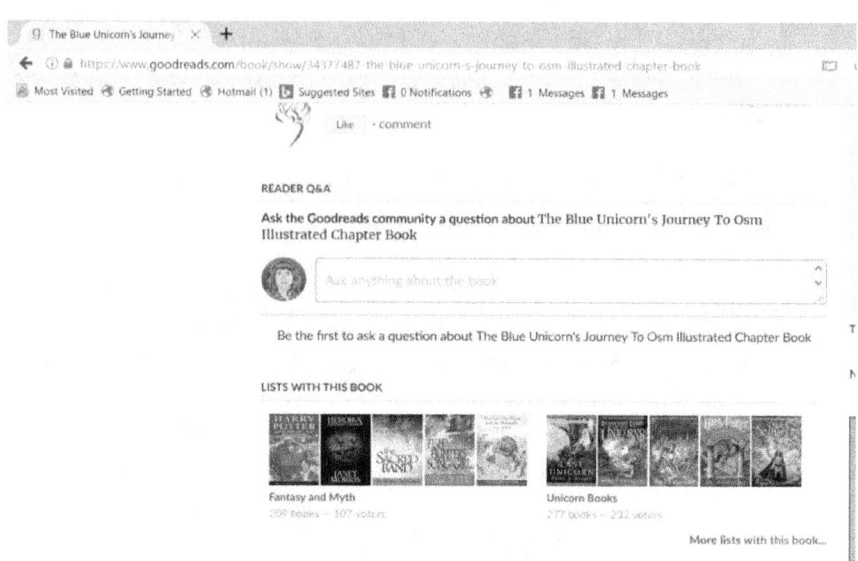

If you click on the More Lists with this book hyperlink, you will see all of the book lists featuring your book.

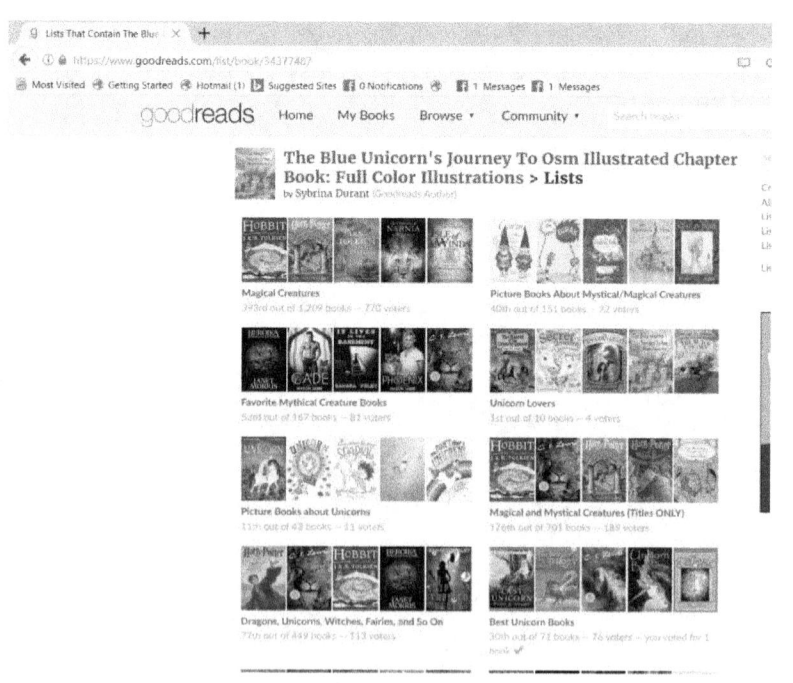

Now that you know about book lists and their value, please
consider helping out a fellow author and vote up The Blue
Unicorn's Journey To Osm on some of the lists at
https://www.goodreads.com/list/book/34377487 .

Note: *Goodreads used to offer an amazing giveaway promotion
service on their site for Free but that all changed in October
2017. Things change so incredibly fast in this industry and one
of the motivating factors of change is money-making
opportunities. Unfortunately for independent authors,
Goodreads has decided that they can charge quite a lot to
advertise Giveaways so this is no longer a free service. Read
more about Goodreads Giveaways in the Paid Advertising
section of this book.*

Other sites similar to GoodReads include Shelfari (Associated
with Amazon, also), Jacket Flap, LibraryThing (nearly 2 million
reader members), Booklikes and Freado. As of 2017, their
giveaways are still free.

Get Book Reviews

There are many bloggers out there who will review the types of books that they enjoy reading for FREE. They are going to read them anyway, so why not read books that authors give them in exchange for reviews. It can be very time consuming to find people to review your books but it can be done. In order for this review process to be FREE for you, only offer electronic book files for review. Preferably PDF files. Otherwise, you'll be spending money on purchasing your own printed books and on postage and it will no longer be considered a FREE review.

That means, don't bother approaching reviewers who say they will only read printed books as you will be wasting your time and theirs. Other things to keep in mind:

1. Only offer your book to a blogger who says they read your style of book.

2. Don't pester a potential reviewer. Only contact them one time. Do not check in to see if they've read the book. If someone has gone to the trouble of actually reviewing your book, they will let you know when and where it has been posted. Most reviewers know that their effort to review your book will bring potential visitors to their site from your sphere of influence. So, if they like your book, they will review it. If they don't, they won't...some things you just have to brush off. Like I've always told my grandkids, "Be a duck...just let the water roll right off your back."

3. If your book is reviewed always thank the reviewer and post a link to their review from your different sites – Facebook, Pinterest, Your webpage, Your Blog, etc.

It is very rare that completely "FREE" reviews are acquired. It can happen, though. Sometimes, a brand new book blogger will give some free reviews, just to have something to post on their

new blog. Other times, you can trade reviews with other
authors and post on each other's blogs or websites. But be
careful with "swapping" reviews. Some people seem to feel the
swaps will be nothing more than mutual flattery, thus virtually
worthless in their minds. You will have to make up your own
mind about this.

Sometimes, you can get a review from someone who has won
your book in a competition.

***Here's a page from my website where I feature reviews
I've written for other Children's Picture book Authors.***
You can visit this page at
*http://www.sybrina.com/index_Childrens_Book_Reviews_By_
Sybrina.htm*

When reviews of your books are posted on other people's blogs or websites, you can link to those reviews from a page you've created for reviews of your books on your book blog or website.

NOTE: *You don't always have to wait for a blogger to notify you that they've posted a review of your book. Set up a Google Alert for your book title and your author name so that you will be notified when your book title is captured by a search bot. Go here to learn how –*

https://support.google.com/alerts/answer/4815696?hl=en

You can also post links to those other blogs and websites from your Facebook, Twitter, Instagram and Pinterest pages.

Here's an example book review page from my website. These are reviews other people have written for my book, "The Blue Unicorn's Journey To Osm Illustrated Book" for teens and older readers. You can visit that page at http://www.sybrinablueunicornbook.com/index_Blue_Unicorn _Book_Reviews.htm

Notice that I only have brief paragraphs of each review. Some are from the very beginning of the review and some start later in the review text. It all depends on what puts your book in the best light. Place a link to the rest of the review in the "Read More" text at the end of the review paragraph.

You can also post links to those other blogs and websites from your Facebook, Twitter and Pinterest pages. Anytime, you can help others out by posting links to their businesses, you're doing a good thing. It will be welcomed and appreciated by the people you share marketing efforts with. The best part is that you can do it all for FREE.

Note 1: You can place a link to all reviews from Amazon for a particular book with a link like this.
https://www.amazon.com/Blue-Unicorns-Journey-Plain-llustrations-ebook/product-reviews/B06XD8KZVJ

Note 2: Sometimes links get broken for some reason or other. Maybe the blogger changed up their previous formatting. Maybe they are using another blogging service. Maybe they no longer have a blog at all. If you do not want to lose the full text of those reviews, you might want to copy and paste them into a Word file that you keep in your computer for future reference. It's a good idea to keep copies for your own inspiration of future book descriptions and other marketing purposes.

Facebook Review Page

If you have an individual Facebook page for your book and you really should, ask reviewers to post their reviews on it. Facebook allows for multiple pages that are linked to your personal profile. You can have a book page, an author page, a store page and many other types of pages. If you want reviews on your book page, you will have to ask reviewers to post them there. You will not be able to do it yourself. Here's my review page for "The Blue Unicorn's Journey To Osm Illustrated Book For Teens" on Facebook.

https://www.facebook.com/pg/The-Blue-Unicorns-Journey-To-Osm-794155627353303/reviews/

Booktube

If you've never heard of Booktube you might want to check it
out. Supposedly, there are over a hundred thousand book
video bloggers or booktubers talking about and reviewing books
on Youtube right now. Go to Youtube and search for booktube
or booktuber or "book vlog" to get thousands of links to video
book bloggers. Most of the booktube vloggers feature their
contact info on their "About" page. If you come across a
booktuber who you think might enjoy your book, send them a
message requesting a review. You never know...they might just
do it.

Anyone can be a Booktuber. If you have a good video camera
and want to give it a try yourself, do it! Just record and upload
to Youtube. Make sure to give your video a hashtag such as
#booktuber or #booktube or #bookvlogger and you will be one
of the growing crowd of video book bloggers.

Pinterest

Oh what a marvelous invention! What the heck did we do
before Pinterest? It is the fastest growing tool available for
sharing information on the internet. As of 2017, 31% of all
internet surfers are spending lots of time browsing on Pinterest
to see what the latest and greatest "stuff" is.   That's about 150
million Pinterest users worldwide.

I, too, enjoy viewing new items posted there several times a
day. If you're not careful you can get carried away clicking on
all the related links. It is quite addictive, thus making it a
valuable tool for book promotion.

If you haven't already joined Pinterest, now is the time to set up
a FREE account for your author activities. Name your profile
Your Name – Author. Create as many boards as you can think of

to draw people in to your area. Have a board for your book
containing excerpts from the book and book reviews. Create
other boards which are related in some aspect to different
facets of your book. Does it take place in Scotland? Start
pinning Scottish items. Is it about unicorns? Start pinning
unicorns? Is it a cook book? Start pinning pictures of the
different recipes in your book.

For example, to promote my book, "Learn To Tie A Tie With The
Rabbit And The Fox" I created a Pinterest board showing lots of
cute kids wearing neckties. Check it out here
**http://www.pinterest.com/sybrinad/learn-to-tie-a-tie-with-
the-rabbit-and-the-fox/**

For "The Blue Unicorn's Journey To Osm Illustrated Book For
Teens" Pinterest board, I have started something new that I call
"Review Quote Pics". Here is a sample of one.

I usually purchase an appropriate image from Dreamstime.com or some other source for the background. If your book is illustrated, you can even use a portion of an illustration as a background. The bottom left corner of my Review Quote Pic always contains the book logo and the bottom right corner always contains the book cover image. In between both of those, I list the quote source. The rest of the upper part of the picture contains the Review Quote. Once created and posted on Pinterest (or Instagram or Facebook), I link the picture from Pinterest to the review itself on Amazon, the blog, Smashwords, Barnes and Nobles or where ever it may be originally posted.

The possibilities for board ideas are endless. Just start and you'll be rolling along before you know it. You can also invite other people (only those you trust who have boards like yours) to pin to your boards. The advantage of doing that is all of their followers will see what they pinned on your board. That could gain more followers for you. You can do all of this for FREE, so get started.

It is also free to join Pinterest as a business. You can even convert an existing account to a business account. One of the many benefits of having a business account is that you can get codes to post your most popular pins on your website or blog.

See an example of that on my website. Look on the right - about 1/ 4 way down the page.

http://www.sybrina.com/index_Nellie_Knows_How_To_Knot_ A_Neck_Scarf.htm.

Go to this webpage to learn more about Pinterest for Business.

https://business.pinterest.com/en

You can also purchase pay per click advertising on Pinterest but of course, that is not free.

Instagram

Another great place to promote your book is on Instagram. Just like Youtube has Booktube, Instagram has Bookstagram. It is an area on Instagram dedicated to people who love books. To make yourself a part of it, simply use the hashtag #bookstagram in your Instagram profile and people will be able to find your posts. Use it in individual posts, too.

Instagram was created for smartphone use. The creators wanted people to take spontaneous pictures and video from their phones and upload directly from their phones. Instagram became wildly popular with people doing just that. That's all well and good but what that means is it is not user friendly at all when working from a laptop or desktop. Most people spend hours creating cool graphics and other advertising material to sell their books. How disappointing not to be able to share them on Instagram. Not to worry...you can still do that but first you must get your graphics from your computer to your phone before you can upload them to Instagram. All you need is a phone/usb charging cord. Connect the cord to both devices (Phone and laptop or phone and desktop) and open Windows Explorer. Your phone will be listed on the left side of the explorer window.   Browse to DCIM/Camera.

I advise doing continuous file maintenance on your camera folder to keep your phone space as clear as possible.

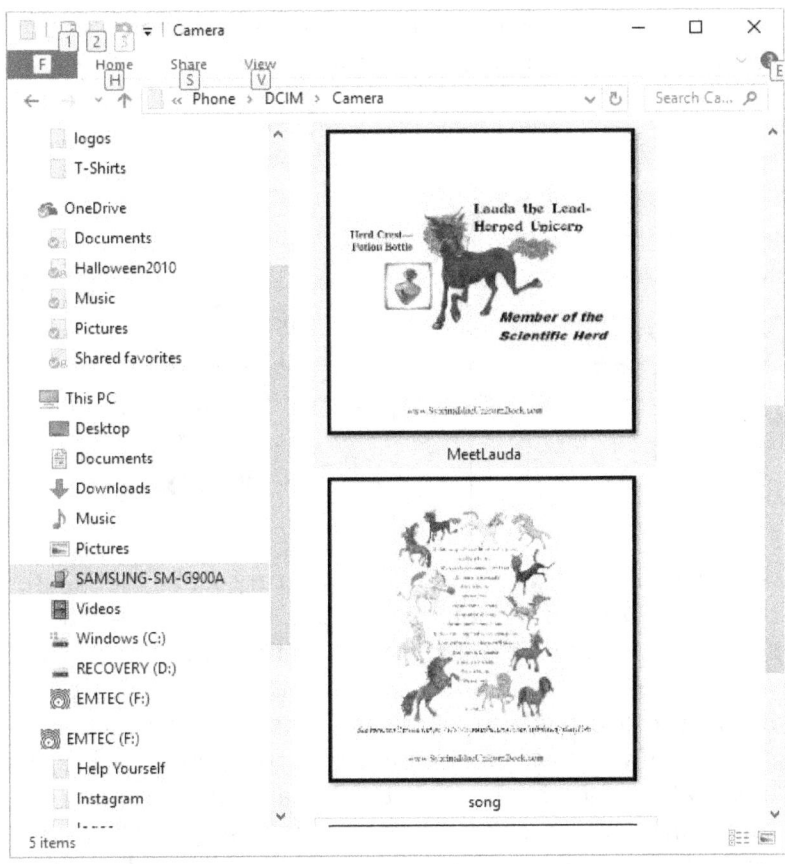

Open a 2nd Windows Explorer window and browse to where you keep your Instagram graphics. Then drag and drop from your computer to your phone.

Visit my Instagram #bookstagram at
https://www.instagram.com/sybrinablueunicorn/ Follow me when you get there!

You will notice that all of my Instagram posts are an exact square. I use a template to create all of the images for my posts to maintain some sort of uniformity in my presentations. If you

look at a lot of bookstagrammers, you will see the same sort of
continuity throughout their presentations.

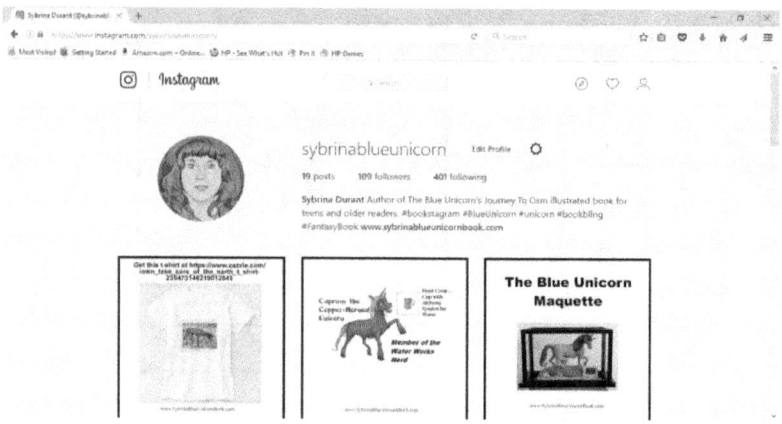

A note about Hashtags – Hashtags are a very useful tool to use
on sites like Facebook, Pinterest, Twitter, Instagram and other
social media sites. A hashtag starts with the # sign and then a
word or phrase. Phrases must not contain spaces in a hashtag.
Hashtags provide links to other posts containing identical
hashtags. If you place hashtags in your posts, people clicking on
them will see all other posts on that social media platform
containing that particular word or phrase. Using hashtags is a
great way for people who didn't know you existed to find your
posts.

Book Trailer

You can hardly find a book these days that doesn't have an
associated book trailer on Youtube or on one of the many other
video sharing sites. Some of the other sites are tumblr,
Dailymotion, flicker, photobucket, Myspace, Vimeo, Snapchat
and others.

This is a cool video sharing site, too,
http://booktrailers.ning.com/

You can post your book trailers on Youtube, too.

To create my book trailer videos, I use Microsoft Office PowerPoint to create the slides for the different images in the video. I'll usually include some slides with notes to the viewer along with pages from the book. Once I have created all of the slides that I want to use, I insert them into Windows Movie Maker program (which can be downloaded for free from *http://www.windows-movie-maker.org/download.html* and then add audio.

Windows Movie Maker program easily converts the file to a movie file that can be uploaded right to Youtube.

Since I write songs for all of my children's books, I usually have the main song playing over the video. My advice is to make your trailer no longer than 1 minute since people have such short attention spans these days. If you don't have your own music, Youtube has a huge selection of music that you can use for free for your video once you upload it to their site.

Here is a book trailer on Youtube with a song I wrote that inspired the book, "Yarashell Abbily And Her Very Messy Room" - *http://youtu.be/1ssHqH3rbQM*.

Here's one where I used a free music track from Youtube. I just love this music! It is the book trailer for Sybrina's Phrase Thesaurus - *http://youtu.be/pWjsZGHp8RE* .

So, get yourself a free Youtube account and start uploading your own Book Trailers and other promotional videos.

You can also get a free Youtube Movie Maker program from... *http://www.makeyoutubevideo.com/download.html*

Learn how to use that program here... *https://youtu.be/Woy9FlOn-xc*

After you've created your video and uploaded it to Youtube, remember to post a link to your book on Amazon or Barnes and Noble or even to your website from the book trailer video page.

Once you have your book trailer, go a step further than Youtube and have your video uploaded to as many sites as possible. Fiverr.com has service providers who will upload your video to as many as 30 video sharing sites for you for $5.00. That's a fantastic deal!

Review Quote Videos

While we're discussing Youtube, you might want to know about something else I've started posting there. These little beauties are about 30 seconds long and I call them Review Quote Videos. You can follow the process above to create the animation for your video. The Review Quote should only be about one to two sentences long. It should include a title like "Review Quote For The Blue Unicorn's Journey To Osm Illustrated Book For Teens By Amazon Reviewer". Next, would be the actual quote and finally an image of the book. The fun part about Youtube is that you can upload a video with no sound. Once the video is finished processing you can add sound from a multitude of choices that are offered on Youtube for FREE.

You can see several samples of Review Quotes for The Blue Unicorn's Journey To Osm here -
https://www.youtube.com/playlist?list=PLybqF-7D4W3GXgRRtTioxMORllrjanX0l

Give Away A Free Sample Chapter Or Even A Free Book!

Giving something away for FREE is the best FREE method of advertising and marketing. If you are a children's picture book author, offer the first 1/3 of your book for

free. If you write romance novels, offer the 1st Chapter for
free. There may even be times, especially if your book is
part of a series, that you might want to offer the entire
first book for free. Whatever you do, make sure to include
enough to make the reader want to purchase the rest of
the book, either in ebook or printed format.

Here's what you do. Use the same method to create your
free sample PDF file that you used to put your book
together. Make a copy of your Microsoft Word or
Publisher document and delete all of the pages at the end
that you don't want to "give" away. Create a new "last"
page for your free sample. This page will contain text
similar to the following:

*Finish reading this book. It is available in Kindle and epub
ebook formats and in soft cover and hard back. Click here
to find out where to get it in your favorite formats. PS: If
you would like to read this book but are low on funds, ask
your local librarian to order and shelve it. The ISBN
number is….*

See a sample Free Book Sample Here

http://www.sybrina.com/YAVMR-ReadSample.pdf

and here

http://www.sybrina.com/MSARead1stChapterFree.pdf

and look below to download an entire book that I've
decided to give away for free…I figure if people love it,
they'll purchase the other 3 volumes.

http://www.phrasethesaurus.com/FreeSPTVol1-MP1.pdf

This is your chance to go all out in promoting your book.
You can place this book sample on your website server,
create a link to it from your books webpage and then you
can place the books sample link absolutely every place
that allows you to place a personal website link. You can
link to it from Facebook, GoodReads, Twitter, Youtube,
every writer's group, every reader's group, every
everywhere than you can think of. You can even link to it
when you're trying to submit your book through library
websites. And the best part about it all is that it costs you
absolutely nothing. Don't forget to write a press release
announcing that you are giving away that free reading
sample or book!

Link Shorteners and Universal Links

You may have noticed that most of the website address
links I've listed in this book so far are pretty long. Now is
the time to let you know about Link Shorteners and
Universal links. A good reason to use link shorteners is
because the new links are so short that parts of them will
never be hidden on sites like Facebook and Twitter. Link
shorteners may be used for every type of web page
address. There are a lot of link shortening sites but these
are the most popular:

https://goo.gl/

https://bitly.com/

https://tinyurl.com/

Universal links, on the other hand are mainly for Amazon web page addresses. They will allow anyone who clicks on that link to go immediately to the book's Amazon page in their country. This is very useful for sales as well as getting reviews from other countries. The service is here - *http://www.booklinker.net/*

Collect Email Addresses

You may not need them right away but eventually, you will find a need for the email address of people who are interested in your books. For instance, you might want to send notices about upcoming sales or other information about your books. If you have a website or a blog, you can place a subscriber form on it for collecting email addresses. Make sure you request both the first and last name of each subscriber because you will need them both if you ever join a newsletter distribution service.

Now, at this point I have to mention that there are some very strict rules these days about sending emails. If you happen to send more than two or three per day with the same subject line, from your regular email, your email provider might send you a warning about SPAM, threatening to take away your rights to send any further emails through them. You don't want that to happen.

So, a huge market has opened up for newsletter distribution service providers which are licensed to verify that you have collected all of the emails you are using only from people who are interested in what you are marketing. There are a very few email/newsletter providers that claim to be free services but in general, they are not free. Some of the ones that offer some limited free services are:

https://www.mailerlite.com/

https://mailchimp.com

https://www.sendinblue.com

https://www.benchmarkemail.com/

https://www.cleverreach.com/en/

Be aware that when you use a free service; that company's branding will show up on all of your emails. You also will not be able to access advanced reporting features or use premium features like automated marketing.

More information is provided below about newsletters and distribution services.

Newsletter subscriber forms usually are free. My web host provider, Doteasy, provides a form so I use theirs. It is just a link that I placed in a simply designed box. The blue box on the right in the picture below is how it looks on my webpage.

When you click on the <u>Sign Up</u> link it will take you to a form page that looks like this.

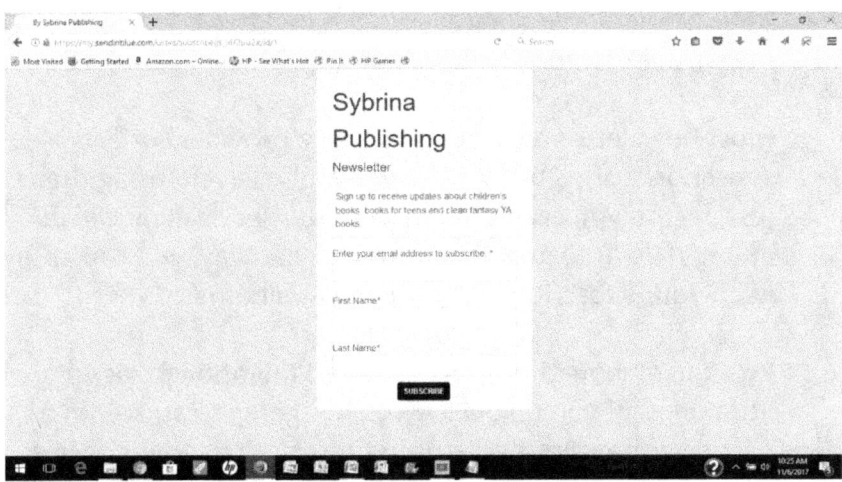

Most website hosts will offer this feature but if you happen to have one that doesn't, there are many others available. Some free ones are below.

https://www.jotform.com

https://www.formsite.com/

If you have a blog rather than a website, there are probably signup form plugins available for your use from the blog host.

Some different blog sites are:

https://wordpress.org/

https://www.blogger.com

https://www.wix.com/

https://penzu.com/

Most newsletter distribution service providers offer subscriber forms but you might want to avoid using theirs just in case you aren't happy with the service you chose and you want to go with another. That way, you can easily keep your subscriber list with you at all times.

You know...now that I've said that, I might backtrack a little on it. If you do decide you are going to stick with a particular newsletter distribution service it would be best to use their sign up form. The reason is because they will not challenge your new subscribers when they actually go through them like they will when you import them via excel files. If you upload new subscribers from other sources, these distribution services are less likely to trust them and sometimes it can cause you all kinds of trouble. You will be less likely of being accused of SPAM if you use the newsletter distribution services Double Opt-In forms.

You can also add any of these Sign Up forms to your books Facebook page. Just click on the learn more button (in

Facebook) and pick Get In Touch | Sign Up. Then, link to
your sign-up form on your website or blog.

My newsletter sign up link is
*https://my.sendinblue.com/users/subscribe/js_id/2uu2k
/id/1*. I'd love for you to subscribe.

Autographs

If you are lucky enough to sell some books, you will surely
be asked for your autograph once in a while. That's easy
enough to do when you are right there with someone who
has purchased a printed book from you. But what if
someone purchased your book from another country or
even just another city where you will never travel. What if
they loved your book so much that they contacted you for
your autograph?

If the book is in print, there are several cool things you can
do. You can have some bookplates printed (they have
sticky backs) and send an autographed one to the
requestor.

You can even print personalized book plates yourself using
the Avery 6-up labels. They are bookplate size.

What if your fan purchased an ebook? Believe it or not
there is a service called Authorgraph.com that's especially
for signing ebooks.

Here's how mine looks there. . .

Authorgraph from Sybrina Durant

Whatever the case may be, if a fan loves your work so much that they ask for your autograph, it's best to accommodate their request. It will guarantee that they will spread the word about your book to others.

Paid Writer's Programs and Services

There is so much more that you can do to produce, publish and promote your books but we've about covered everything that is FREE.

Book Creation Programs

In the "Free" section of this book I told you that I use Microsoft Publisher for all of my book creation. If you decide you would like to purchase that program, go to *https://www.microsoft.com/en-us/store/b/office?icid=CNavSoftwareOffice&activetab=tab%3ahomeorpersonal* to check out the offerings from Microsoft.

There are many other book creation programs available that you might prefer. You can find detailed information and buy links for Scrivner, Google Docs, Ulysses and Vellum here - *https://thewritepractice.com/best-book-writing-software/* You will also get info about several grammar and style checkers.

Learn about YWriter, Fast Pencil's Book Writer, Ommwriter, Noilsi, and Sigil here - *http://authorunlimited.com/best-writing-software/*

This article has reviews for a lot more writing programs. Some look really fun, like StoryShop. That one will help you create worlds, elements, and characters in your novels. The article is well worth the read - *https://kindlepreneur.com/best-book-writing-software/*

If you are artistic and would like to create your own artwork for your book, there are a lot of programs available for creating professional looking illustrations. All of the listings in this article are supposedly free and they may be – at first. Usually, you will end up paying something to get the fully functional program. *https://beebom.com/best-free-photoshop-alternatives/*

Book Production

If you are not into the entire creation process listed in the last
section, never fear. You can write or design your book and then
pay to have it formatted. Heck, you can even provide an outline
and summary to a ghost writer and they will write a book for
you!

Maybe you are not artistic but your book needs lots of
illustrations or book cover design. Never fear, there are many
great artists in the world hoping you'll find them for your
project. So many talented people are out there, it will make
your head spin.

All books need to be edited by someone else besides you.
There are reasonably priced editors for every type of book.
Every printed book must have companion ebooks nowadays.
There are conversion services which can turn your electronic
files into epub, mobi and other file formats.

Want your book to be produced in audio format? Need a book
trailer to promote your book? There are many service providers
available to do all of these things for you.

I have used every service from Fiverr to People Per Hour to
Upwork because I can purchase services from them at
reasonable prices. I even became acquainted with the
illustrator for "The Blue Unicorn's Journey To Osm" in a
Facebook group for writers and illustrators.

There are also many companies out there which specialize in
these services but they generally charge higher prices. Just do
the research and pick the services that are within your budget
and which seem right for your project.

Services like Fiverr, People Per Hour and Upwork are perfect for
people on limited budgets. When you don't have much money

to spend they are great places to find super talented people, some who are just honing their skills and others who already have years of expertise but don't have jobs with well known companies in their particular industry. I think of it as eating at a mom and pop place versus a fine dining establishment. Both provide nourishment and taste to satisfy the pallet. Not everyone can afford to purchase a meal prepared by a renowned chef but nearly everyone can afford a meal outside the home from time to time. Paying less for a service does not mean that it is inferior. Just as the services provided by workers on Upwork or People Per Hour or even on Fiverr are not inferior to those at more expensive firms. We should consider ourselves fortunate that we have many options in every arena of life.

Here's a list of quite a few other service provider sites that are reasonably priced.

https://www.freelancer.com/

https://www.fieldnation.com/

http://www.ifreelance.com/

http://www.freelancewritinggigs.com/ (for editors and ghostwriting)

https://www.collegerecruiter.com

http://www.guru.com

Here's a website that lists 50 freelance websites - *http://www.hongkiat.com/blog/50-freelance-job-sites-for-designers-programmers-best-of/*

Book Illustrators

I have utilized the services of many different illustrators for many different aspects of book projects.

I was fortunate to come across Donna Marie Naval, from the Philippines, on Odesk (Now Upwork). She illustrated my very first book, "Learn To Tie A Tie With The Rabbit And The Fox" and truly brought my ideas to life in a way that I could never have imagined possible...except that the fox in the story actually looks more like a wolf, but that is my fault more than hers. I just didn't feel comfortable asking her to change it. And actually, I like the look...it's definitely a conversation starter.

That was before I realized how very important it is to actually send pictures of actual animals and other objects to illustrators in foreign countries.

Lesson Learned: If something doesn't look right to you, speak up. Let the illustrator know if you want something changed. They will definitely accommodate you. I was just being overly sensitive to hurting her feelings when it actually would not have.

Most of the service providers on services like Upwork (merged from Elance and Odesk) do know how to communicate in English to some extent. Even if they don't know it very well and you don't know their language at all, communication is possible with the help of tools like Google translator and such. You do need to be acutely aware, though, that the message may not always come across exactly as it should.

Donna and I were both completely new to the process of book production and we made a few mistakes together. Besides not asking her to fix the fox, I was under the misconception that I needed both CMYK, for the printed book and RGB for the ebook and she didn't know that I didn't. It turns out that the RGB file

can be converted to CMYK when creating the PDF file so now, I
just ask for RGB jpg files.

Another mistake I made in my first effort was not asking the
illustrator to provide a set of jpgs with the text plus a set
containing no text. If you hire an illustrator, make certain you
include that as part of the deliverables in the description of your
project. Otherwise, it may cost you more later.

Take a look at Donna Marie's work here –

*http://www.sybrina.com/index_Rabbit_Fox_Story_Listen_To_
Song_For_Free.htm* .

and here…

*http://www.sybrina.com/index_Learn_To_Knot_A_Neck_Scarf
_With_The_Rabbit_And_The_Fox_Book.htm*

Sara Wilson and about 50 other artists submitted their
proposals to work on "Yarashell Abbily and Her Very Messy
Room" through Elance (now Upwork). I chose her because I
absolutely fell in love with the artwork in her portfolio. Her
joyful rendition of Yarashell makes me smile every time I look at
her.

Look at her work here –

*http://www.sybrina.com/index_Yarashell_Abbily_and_Her_V
ery_Messy_Room_Book_Info.htm*

I came across Enrique Vignolo from Argentina on Linked In.
Sandi Johnson was looking for an illustrator to perfectly portray
her character, Dorp the Scottish Dragon in a "Lone Star Story". I
hired Enrique because his artwork had so much depth to it.
Every single picture is full of fun things to catch a child's eye. It

reminded me of the work of the famous children's book
illustrator, Richard Scarry.

See samples from that book here –

*http://www.sybrina.com/index_Dorp_The_Scottish_Dragon_A
_Lone_Star_Story_Book.htm*
I liked Enrique's artwork so much that I hired him again to
illustrate my book, "Nellie Knows How To Knot A Neck Scarf".
See it here -

*http://www.sybrina.com/index_Nellie_Knows_How_To_Knot_
A_Neck_Scarf.htm*

Enrique is in the process of working on my newest tie a tie book
which will be a companion book to Nellie's. It will be called Ned
Knows How To Knot A Neck Tie.

Note: *Elance and Odesk merged into a new company named
Upwork. To join, go to* ***https://www.upwork.com/****.*

When working with an illustrator who you will most likely never
meet in person, it is best to provide as much detail for each
picture as possible to that person. Of course, you can always
Skype or use a similar tool to speak face to face but I don't really
care to do that.

For my children's books, I will create a complete mock up for
the book using Microsoft Powerpoint or Microsoft Publisher.
You could even do it all by hand, then scan the pages to PDF file.
In my file for the artist, I'll include pictures of items that I want
in the book on each page, along with the accompanying text. I'll
also include detailed notes to the artist on each page. It is vital
that you present as much information to the illustrator as
humanly possible so that you will have a more likely chance of
being pleased with the final outcome.

Here is an example of a sample page I sent to the illustrator for a counting book that I recently produced.

This illustrator is from India. I found her through Elance. Her name is Parbbonni. I found these pictures to send her on Dreamstime.com.

Note To Artist:

Page 2 of the book—Every page of the book containing numbers will have one of the children from the book cover interacting with the number somehow. I leave that up to your imagination.

Page 2 is for the number 1. The first picture will be 1 sheep (or lamb). Make it look as close as possible to this lamb.

I would like for this book to be in all bold primary colors. Make the colors for the numbers and the animals complement each other on every page. I wasn't able to do that in all of the examples.

NOTE about all the animals in this book: Try to make them all look like they belong together in this book. What ever your style is, try to keep it through all pages of the book.

***Here's what the page from the book "1, 2, 3 Count With
Me" looked like after Parbbonni had finished with it.*** As
you can see, there are a couple of things that are different from
my original instructions but I liked them enough to keep them.
Sometimes the artist knows best. Visit
http://www.sybrina.com/index_123_Count_With_Me_Co
unt_to_10_and_back_again.htm to hear the
accompanying song for this book. Your kids will love it.

For 'The Blue Unicorn's Journey To Osm Illustrated Book For
Teens", I also sent massive amounts of go-by pictures to the
artist, Sudipta Dasgupta. In addition to the "inspiration"
pictures, I also provided what could almost be described as a
screen play for each scene like the one below.

Chapter 4 Illustration 1

Characters in picture - Ghel, Iown, Style, Cornum, Tinam,
Cuprum, Dr. Zinko, Lauda, Silubhra and Nix

This illustration is in the Great Room/dining room of the
Halstable. Ghel and Iown are in the foreground. Ghel is sitting
on a stool and Iown is standing next to her. Ghel is pushing
food around on her plate. She looks very sad. Iown is making a
funny face at her. Cornum and Style look like they're arguing.
The other unicorns can be doing whatever you want them to
do.

There are different sized tin cans brimming over with food all up
and down the table. Some are tall, some short, some wide,
some flat. Show the tops of the tin cans rolled back or open in
different ways. There is no meat on the table...just fruits,
vegetables and breads. Other unicorns are sitting on both sides
of the table eating off of plates with forks between their split
hooves. There can be cups or goblets at each place setting.
There can also be some kind of centerpiece on the table.

Off to the left side of the room is a big double door that goes
out to the Halstable Courtyard. Off to the right side of the room
is an open kitchen. Decorate the rest of the room however
you'd like.

I also provided the complete text for that chapter so that he
could have the complete context.

Below is the final illustration for that scene.

*Sudipta Dasgupta's final Illustration for Chapter 4,
Illustration 1 from "The Blue Unicorn's Journey To Osm
Illustrated Book For Teens". (Sorry, you can't see this pic
in color in this printed book.)*

*Here's the black and white "wood cut look" version of the
same picture.*

Don't you love it!

The best part about working with a service provider from a
company like Upwork is that those websites are set up so that
you can pay per project or by the hour. I always choose to pay
per project. Paying by hour could potentially run it to a lot of
extra money being spent. If you're really happy with the final
product, it's easy to give bonuses, through these services, too.

To get a project started, simply post your project details on the
website and within an hour, many illustrators begin presenting
their portfolios to you for review. Once you select an illustrator,
you will do all of your business with them through those sites. It
is a safe way to do business.

When working with artists from sites like LinkedIn or Facebook,
you are dealing directly with the artist, with no arbiter, so the
level of trust between you must be very high. When working
with an individual, it is a good idea for both parties to have
Paypal accounts for paying and receiving money. There are
other payment services available now besides Paypal. Just
make sure you pick one with global access.

As with most of the other online services listed in this book, you
must have a bank account in order to be paid by Paypal but you
just need a linked credit card to make payments through Paypal.

Note: *When you hire an illustrator to create the images for your
book, always request 2 final deliverables. The first should
contain the text (if the artist is providing the text) on the jpg
images and the second should have no text at all. I recommend
doing this because you may want to later have your book
translated into different foreign languages. It will be a lot easier
to do so when you have a separate jpg of each page with no
text. For children's illustrated books you might also wish to
request black and white outlined images, too, since coloring
books are so popular with kids.*

If you work with an illustrator outside of Upwork or some other service provider, sign up for a free file exchange service like Dropbox.com so that you may send and receive large files with no trouble. There are many other free file exchange services. Just do a search on "best free large file transfer sites".

Graphic Images – There are many places to acquire fantastic graphic images to use as go-bys or inspiration for your artist or for many other reasons. I've already mentioned that my favorite is *https://www.dreamstime.com/.* It does not require you to become a member. Most others do.   Some other places to get great graphic images are

https://www.stockfreeimages.com/

http://www.freedigitalphotos.net/

https://www.bigstockphoto.com/

Many of these places also offer video files and there are other places that offer audio files that can be used as sound effects. Check out *https://www.audioblocks.com/* and *http://www.freesfx.co.uk/* for some fun sounds.

Book Covers

If you are a romance book writer, I will recommend *http://telltalebookcovers.weebly.com/.*

I have used their services for my sister's romance novels and they have some fantastic pre-made book designs. They will even customize them for you. Take a look at the book cover designs I purchased from them here.

http://www.sybrina.com/index_Retail_Catalog_Regency_Romance_by_Gina_Rose.htm

Don't stop with them, though. Do a search on premade book covers and you will find lots of companies offering some fantastic designs for you to customize for every type of book.

Some others to check out are

https://www.selfpubbookcovers.com/

http://www.creativindiecovers.com/

http://www.creativeparamita.com/premade-book-covers/

https://thebookcoverdesigner.com/product-category/premade-book-covers/

http://www.thecovercollection.com/

Many of these services offer custom cover design also.

Book Editing

You can find book editors at all the services listed above and at specialty companies, too. On Fiverr, you can find a really good editor for $5.00 per 2,500 words. Upwork service providers are a little bit higher. Specialty companies may charge as much as a couple hundred dollars per hour. My advice, as usual, is do your research.

Indexing

There are many types of books which really need a good index, to help the reader locate information quickly. These could be cook books, business books, reference books and others. There is software you can purchase to do your own indexing or you can hire an indexing service. There's even a society for indexers that offers some great information on the topic. Read here *https://www.asindexing.org/about-indexing/frequently-asked-questions/*

More Information About Music

I mentioned earlier that I write songs for most of my children's books. I didn't mention that I am not a musician! Just like anything else I've ever involved myself in; I haven't let that lack of ability slow me down too much. You don't have to, either.

Here's my process for creating music.

First, I write the song lyrics and record them. I usually have a melody in my head about the same time that the lyrics are there. You can use any number of devices these days to capture yourself singing those lyrics with the melody you've come up with. The key is to record on a device which creates an mp3 file. You can purchase little digital recorders very inexpensively these days. Most computers have pretty sophisticated built in microphones and some even come with recording features.

However you decide to do it, make sure you end up with an mp3 file so that you will have it to upload to the person who will create the instrumentals. Also, type out the lyrics on Notepad or Microsoft Word. You will need to provide that to the music composer, too.

Second, find a likely candidate to create your instrumental. I use 3 different online sources for most of my songs. They are Upwork, Fiverr and PeoplePerHour. At whichever site you pick to post your project, you will write a description for your song project, upload the mp3 file and lyric file and list how much you are willing to pay for the finished product. Once you post the project, potential candidates will submit their proposals with samples of their work. You will pick the one whose style most appeals to you for the price you have stated. Using this method, most of my instrumentals have cost less than $50.00.

For that price, I request an mp3 with vocals (so that I can
practice singing the song) and an mp3 without (so that I can add
my voice to the instrumental later).

Once you have the instrumental, there are several methods for
adding your voice. I use a program called Mixcraft. It is very
easy to use. I import the instrumental into the program and
then I add my voice. As I stated, many computers now have
very sophisticated internal microphones. I simply sit at my desk
and sing towards the computer monitor (where the microphone
is located). After my voice has been recorded, I import it into
the Mixcraft program and use the special effects features to
enhance or improve the quality of the vocals. Once everything
is exactly as I want it to sound, I mix it all down to .wav and
.mp3 format. You can purchase the Mixcraft program for less
than $100.00 online or even at a store like BestBuy. There are
many compatible programs available for producing music.

How To Use The MP3 File

After you have an mp3 file for your finished song, you can use it
for any purpose you wish. For example, you can use it for your
book trailer. You can link to it from the book page of your
website so that people can hear it for FREE. You can offer it to
the public for sale through Itunes and for streaming through a
myriad of music services like IHeartRadio.com. Here's the best
method for offering your song to the public for sale.

Join a music licensing service. TuneCore.com is your best bet
for registering, licensing and distributing your music and for
getting paid for any sale or stream of your song from anywhere
in the world. In fact, TuneCore will even register your
compositions with music performance licensing organizations
like BMI (*http://www.bmi.com/about*), ASCAP
(*http://www.ascap.com/about/*), SESAC
(*http://www.sesac.com/*), or SOCAN (*http://www.socan.ca/*).

These are the organizations that make sure you, the songwriter or artist, get paid when your song is played in a public space, like a shopping mall or a restaurant or many other places.

Register with Tunecore and they will take care of all of that for you. Read all about TuneCore services at *http://www.tunecore.com/index/sell_your_music* .

Have you created an audio file of you reading your book yet? If you have, make sure you link it from the book page. Getting to hear the book will cause a lot of people to want to buy it. You can register this with Tunecore, also.

Note: *The reason I told you to save your song file as a .wav is because Tunecore does not allow uploads of mp3s.*

Audio Books

One of my books, "The Blue Unicorn's Journey To Osm, is available as an Audio Book. Since this book is distributed to Amazon through ACX.com and the audio is an exact narration of the ebook, both books are linked together on the Amazon sales pages. In addition to a "Look Inside" reading sample of the book, there is also an Audio sample on the same book sales page.

I do not recommend doing the narration yourself unless you have access to very good recording equipment and the proper environment for sound. The audio book distribution services are very, very picky about their specifications being followed exactly as written. Also, make certain that narration follows the story word-for-word so that it may be eligible for Amazon's Whisper-sync program. That way, readers will be able to read along with the audio on their Kindles. ACX.com is the distributor for audio books via Amazon, Itunes and Audible.com.

Each chapter must be uploaded individually and you will have to also have an opening, closing and a sample audio clip.

You can select a narrator through ACX or you can use an outside narrator.

There are two ways to sign up with ACX. One is an exclusive contract. The other is non-exclusive and it allows you to make your audio book available through other sources. You will receive less royalty income if you do not make the contract exclusive but the advantages of being able to sell your audio book in other ways out-weigh any potential income you might miss out on from ACX. *http://www.acx.com/*

Another great audio distribution company is Author's Republic. They distribute to Audiobooks.com, Audible, iTunes, Amazon, Scribd, Downpour, Barnes & Noble, Nook, Overdrive (libraries), Hoopla (libraries), 3M (libraries), Baker & Taylor (libraries), TuneIn, AudiobookStore.com, and more.
https://www.authorsrepublic.com

You can upload the same files to Authors Republic that you uploaded to ACX. I use both services just to make certain that I get the most benefit from each situation.

Once you have an audio book, you can try to get reviews by giving away codes from Audible.com. There are promotional sites set up especially for this purpose. Some are listed below.

http://audiobookjungle.com/about/review-policy/

https://audiobookboom.com/authors

http://audiothing.blogspot.com.au/

http://audiobookjukebox.squarespace.com/solid-gold-reviewer-program/

https://audiobookreviewer.com/

http://audiobookradio.net/

https://www.audiofilemagazine.com/contact/

http://audavoxx.com/

EverythingAudiobooksE.A.R.S Facebook group -
https://www.facebook.com/groups/EverythingAudiobooksE.A.R.S/ Note: You will probably need to go ahead and log into Facebook and just search for the group name for this and any other Facebook links.

Audiobook Promos for Authors Facebook Group -
https://www.facebook.com/groups/1014732691885069/

Narrators for Audio Books

Fiverr.com is a fantastic source for audio book narrators. When I first decided to create my audio book, I thought I would like to have a different narrator for the voice of each character in the book. I actually have all of them ready-to-go in mp3 files but because of ACX's strict specifications for sound, I dropped the idea of trying to mix all of the character voices with my overall narrator's voice. There were just too many variations in background noise and recording levels.

I decided to go with the overall narrator for the entire book and I am very glad I did. He did an amazing job acting out the voices of over 30 characters. His name is Troy W. Hudson and you can watch him discussing his voice-over process here if you want to. *https://youtu.be/_qh6KSKPE1I* You can hear him narrating a sample of the book here. *https://www.amazon.com/Blue-Unicorns-Journey-Osm/dp/B071SDJQNW*

Book Publishing

Since CreateSpace does not offer the ability to publish hard cover books, I personally utilize the services of Lightning Source for that. Besides CreateSpace, Lightning Source/Ingram is the other self-publishing industry giant. Lightning Source is a little more difficult to deal with than CreateSpace; and they are definitely not FREE but they offer some advantages...like hard cover books . . .which are listed for sale on Amazon.com.

I registered as a publisher with Lightning Source several years ago, before Ingram came out with Ingram Spark. In simple terms, Lightning Source is for publishers of many books. Ingram Spark is for individual self-publishers with few books.

Lightning Source and Ingram Spark both charge set up fees for each individual book. (LS is about $89.00 and IS is about $49.00

per book.) They also charge a yearly fee of about $60.00 to catalog a book. You will have to provide your own ISBN numbers. Many people believe that Lightening Source and Ingram Spark print superior quality books over CreateSpace. Their international shipping also encompasses more foreign countries. Both offer the same shipping destinations in the US, though. If you want to publish hard cover and epub versions of your book, I recommend that you set up an account for yourself through Ingram Spark.

https://www.ingramspark.com/

Everyone will not agree with me on this but I recommend also publishing a 2nd soft cover version of your book through them. Remember, you will have to have your own ISBN numbers to publish through Lightening Source. Publishing through them will insure that your print books are distributed to more than 39,000 retailers, libraries, schools, internet commerce companies, and other channel partners, including Amazon, Barnes & Noble, Chapters/Indigo (Canada), and other well-known book retailers and wholesalers around the world. They will distribute your epub books to over 70 ebook partners including Apple, Barnes & Noble and Library.com.

One benefit of Ingram Spark distributing your book to Amazon is that your hard copy book will be available for sale on Amazon right alongside your CreateSpace printed book and Kindle ebook. Your epub book will not be available on Amazon, though. But it will be available on Barnes and Noble.com as a Nook book.

If you are publishing through Lightening Source, remember to select the option making your wholesale books returnable. If you don't, major brick and mortar retailers will not be willing to stock your book in their stores. You do not have to remember to do this when publishing through Ingram Spark because they will automatically select that option for you.

There are many other services besides CreateSpace and Ingram
Spark available which will help you with some or most of the
aspects of producing, publishing and distributing your printed
book and ebooks. Some of the better known ones are
Bookbaby, LuLu, IUniverse, and Blurb. Look each one up and do
your own research to decide if any of these are preferable to
CreateSpace or Ingram Spark for your needs.

Epub Conversions

I used to use Smashwords exclusively to distribute my epub
books until I discovered that Ingram Spark will do that at the
same time that they distribute your print book. I am not going
to switch my current books, any time soon, from there to
Ingram Spark. One reason is because Smashwords distributes
ebooks to Overdrive, which supplies ebooks to libraries and
Ingram Spark doesn't yet. In fact, right now, I still need to
distribute to Overdrive through Smashwords.

Though there are programs available for converting book files
from either Microsoft Word or PDF (for fully illustrated books)
to epub format, I utilize a service provider for mine. It is just so
much easier not to have to do it myself because there can be a
lot of formatting and indexing involved. Once I have an epub
file, I upload it to Ingram Spark or Smashwords. Ingram Spark
charges a fee for this. Smashwords does not.

One very, very important thing to be aware of is that the
maximum file size for an epub is 10MB. Most illustrated books
are huge file sizes so you need to make the conversion service
provider aware of any applicable rules before they get to work
on a conversion. Most services will be able to compress the file
small enough to be approved by Smashwords or Ingram Spark.
This compression does not seem to affect the quality of the
images.

Smashwords has a rigid requirement that they be listed as the book publisher on the copyright page. So, if you are publishing your epub book through them, you will need to request that your conversion service provide 2 epub files for you – 1 with the Smashwords notice and 1 without. You will use the one that does not have the notification in very many other places, so don't forget to request it.

One great thing about epub files is that Table of Contents and Indexes can be linked to paragraph headings throughout the book. This is a fantastic feature for many different types of books. For instance, the Kindle version of one of my books, Sybrina's Phrase Thesaurus, *http://www.phrasethesaurus.com/*, is somewhat cumbersome and dissatisfying to use while the epub version is a dream.

Kindle books lose any linking that might have originally been in the PDF file in their conversion process unless you upload an actual Word Document to KDP. Unfortunately the formatting for these Kindle books can look pretty terrible but you will be able to retain all hyperlinks. Epub conversion services make certain those links are maintained.

Note: *For a fee, you could pay a conversion service to create an HTML file to convert to a .mobi file that contains linking and then you could replace your old Kindle file with that. Mobi is the file format that Kindle uses. More than likely you'd have to provide the original file (not a PDF) for this type of conversion.*

Check out the Smashwords epub version of Sybrina's Phrase Thesaurus – Volume 4, here –

https://www.smashwords.com/books/view/416546

If you do a search on the internet, you will find that most places charge well over $150.00 to convert a word doc or pdf file to epub. I have used conversion services from Fiverr.com that charge less than half that price plus provide excellent quality products. Never be afraid to think out of the box when trying to track down great service providers with reasonable prices. There are many places that allow you to upload your own epub files. Some even let you upload .doc, .rtf, .pdf and .html files. Some of the bigger epub distributors are smashwords.com, draft2digital.com, play.google.com, writinglife.kobobooks.com, nookpress.com (for Barnes and Noble) and itunesconnect.apple.com (but you will need the ITunes application and MAC software for this).

My advice is to go with Smashwords since they will distribute your epub file to all of those just mentioned epub aggregators and more. One important thing to note is that if you publish your ebook on Smashwords, your book will be distributed to Overdrive. Overdrive is the online library source that most libraries utilize for ebooks. All you need is a library card to check out ebooks from Overdrive. At this writing, Ingram Spark does not appear to distribute to Overdrive.

Book Translation Services

I have had 1 of my books translated into 3 different languages. "Learn To Tie A Tie With The Rabbit And The Fox" has been translated into Spanish, Tagalog (Philippino) and Simplified Chinese. I trust two of the translations enough to have published them.

You can learn more about them here

http://www.sybrina.com/index_Spanish_Language_Rabbit_Fox_Story_Listen_To_Song_For_Free.htm and here

http://www.sybrina.com/index_Tagalog_Language_Rabbit_Fox_Story_Listen_To_Song_For_Free.htm .

The Simplified Chinese version, on the other hand, makes me very uncomfortable. My usual method for translations is to FIRST hire 1 translator. Once they have completed their translation, I send that file to a SECOND person to translate it back to English. If everything looks as it should, I publish the book in the translated language.

When I tried the same thing with the Chinese language book, I got a bunch of garbledy-goop back...several times. I must admit I spent way too much money going back and forth trying to get a translation that I felt comfortable with. After 5 tries, I decided to shelve the Simplified Chinese version of the book until some future time.

I've always found translators through Elance and Odesk (Now Upwork). But I think if I try the Chinese book translation again, next time I'll go with a service recommended by the Independent Book Publishers Association (IBPA - *http://www.ibpa-online.org/*) or some other trusted source.

One they highly recommend is Rancho Park Publishing - *http://www.ranchopark.com/translation.htm*

Another good possibility might be Translation By Design - *http://www.translationbydesign.com/services/translation*

Note: *An important note about Amazon is that they do not provide Kindle books in all languages. Tagalog is one language they do not deal with so the Philippino (Tagalog) version of my book "Learn To Tie A Tie With The Rabbit And The Fox" is only available in Tagalog as a printed book on Amazon. I had no problem with the epub conversion to that language and it is available on Barnes and Noble, Itunes, Kobo and other epub publishers.*

Printed Book Distributors and Wholesalers

As I've mentioned previously, CreateSpace and Ingram Spark offer great distribution platforms for both printed and electronic books. BookBaby, LuLu, IUniverse, BookWhirl, Blurb and many others also offer good printed and ebook distribution networks to get your book into the marketplace.

My personal experience with BookBaby

A few years ago, when I first got started, I knew absolutely nothing about the book business. Doing an internet search, I came across BookBaby. At the time, they did not offer print on demand (POD) but they did offer ebook distribution to many online book stores such as Amazon and Barnes & Noble. They even converted to Kindle format (mobi) and to epub formats so I decided to go with them for my first ebook, "Learn To Tie A Tie With The Rabbit And The Fox". This was long before I became aware of CreateSpace, which I much prefer.

If you do decide to use a paid publishing service, BookBaby will be about the same as any other, now that they offer POD. Like the others mentioned above, for a pretty penny, they will make your title available to online bookstores, libraries and for wholesale ordering through Ingram, Baker & Taylor and many others. But as I've said many times, there is no good reason to pay a service to make your soft cover book available on Amazon and to their distribution partners when you can do it for free by yourself.

There are other types of book distributors or fulfillment companies which are very difficult to engage. These are the types of companies who have representatives who work as salesmen who literally take your books around to stores to try to gain shelf space for it. As with acquiring the interest of a large book publishing company, most of those types of companies will not deal with anyone who has not already proven they can sell lots of their own books themselves. But as hard as this task might be, I certainly won't discourage you from trying to get one interested in distributing your book for you.

You can find a great contact list to start with at *https://en.wikipedia.org/wiki/List_of_book_distributors*.

One to consider trying to sign your book with is *http://www.ipgbook.com/* - Independent Publisher's Group is the original and second largest independent book distributor in the United States.

Get a Block of ISBN Numbers

If you want to use your own ISBN numbers you should purchase and register them with *http://www.myidentifiers.com*.

This is the website address for Bowker Identifier Services, the only official U.S. ISBN Agency. In 2017, 1 ISBN number costs $125.00. Yes, you read that right! However, you can purchase a block of 100 ISBN numbers for $575.00 which reduces the cost to $5.75 per ISBN number. It's a lot to pay upfront but you might decide it is worth the initial cost if you decide to publish through other sources beyond CreateSpace and if you have a lot of books in your backlog to publish. You will want to weigh the options and make the decision which works best for you in the long run.

Publicity, Marketing and Advertising

Everywhere you present your book is an opportunity for publicity. Whether it's on Goodreads, Twitter, Instagram, Facebook, your website; at an arts and crafts fair, a book fair; or in an advertisement or a book trailer, wherever the book is seen by someone, it is getting publicity.

Note: *If you can't or don't want to create a book trailer
yourself, you can purchase one starting at around $50.00 and
you can even pay up to $1,000.00 or more. I purchased the
white board book trailer for my Phrase Thesaurus book through
PeoplePerHour.com for $50.00.*

*Check it out at **https://youtu.be/pWjsZGHp8RE** .*

*Even better, I purchased a white board type of book trailer for
The Blue Unicorn's Journey To Osm Coloring book. It cost a little
bit more but it is absolutely awesome. This service provider
started out with a black and white picture from the coloring
book and matched it with the same color picture from the
illustrated book so that it looks like she is painting the picture as
she goes through the video. Take a look at it at*
https://youtu.be/TmXUi0hljDk

There is never a moment where you should feel comfortable
enough to stop publicizing or marketing your book. Email and
Snail Mail are both great sources for book marketing. Most
email services charge by how many emails you send out per
month. Most of them expect you to provide your own email
lists but you can purchase all sorts of lists in every category
imaginable. Some services that will actually send your emails
out to their specialized email lists are

http://www.aplustraffic.com/email.html

http://webtraffic21.com/

http://www.advertyze.com/

and *http://www.blast4traffic.com/*

The same goes for mailing label lists for printed material. I have
to admit that I don't really involve myself in this type of email
marketing much, mainly because it is actually pretty expensive

and so many rules apply. I prefer post card marketing because people tend to save post cards for products they're interested in whereas an unsolicited email is likely to land in a junk mail folder, never to be seen. Plus you can use post cards as hand outs when exhibiting or elsewhere. Regardless of my opinion on the subject, you should do the research to see what appeals to you.

Speaking of hand outs, make sure you have lots of fliers, post cards, business cards, book marks and even copies of your books to give away when appropriate. Always carry a copy of your book with you. You never know when you might have an opportunity to talk about it with someone.

There are so many ways to advertise your book these days. The amount of advertising depends on how much money you are willing or able to spend.

You can actually advertise on the radio for around $2,000.00 for a week of exposure. If you're interested, here's a pretty good article on the subject. ***https://fitsmallbusiness.com/radio-advertising/***

Most advertising in local children's business directories will cost around $300.00 a month for a quarter page ad. A quarter page ad in a national weekly magazines might cost $50,000.00 a week!

You can have your book listed in a cooperative book sales catalog for under $200.00 for a quarter page ad. Many author and publisher groups offer opportunities for members to buy book selling space in their member catalogs. Just do a google search on "cooperative book sales catalog" to find lots of co-op opportunities.

You can purchase a 1"x2" banner ad on a blog for $100.00 a month.

You can pay for a virtual book tour of blogs for a hundred bucks or so.

You can bid for ad space on Google and Yahoo and Bing for a few cents per click. The possibilities are endless if you have the money to spend.

That's why I recommend that you try to stick with the FREE stuff. It can take you pretty far. Whatever you do, you must have an Author website or blog to send potential customers to from any advertising sources that you use.

Author Website and/or Blog

I highly recommend that you build a website. This is the place
to promote all of your books and book related merchandise plus
all of the services you come up with to provide for others. You
will be surprised just how creative you might get in the future.

For instance, you might want to have website pages directed at
schools. Here you would place information about yourself, your
book, the author program you provide and other details to
encourage school librarians or teachers to hire you. I don't have
a particular page on my website for that yet. With a full time
job, I am not available to do presentations during the day.
Maybe once I retire from my full time job that will be part of my
marketing plan. If it is something you are ready for you can find
lots of examples by searching "school visits by children's
authors" on your favorite search engine.

If you're interested in learning more about author visits to
schools, you can start here *http://schoolvisitexperts.com/*

You can devote separate pages on your website for posting
book reviews for other author's books by you as well as for
reviews by others about your books.

Here is a review page for one of my books on my website.
*http://www.sybrina.com/index_Book_Reviews_For_Learn_To
_Tie_A_Tie_With_The_Rabbit_And_The_Fox.htm*

You can create catalog pages for all of your books plus
individual web pages for each book. It is one of the most cost
effective means of marketing because you can send all contacts
to that webpage for expansive information about you and your
books. Make sure to create 2 different catalog pages. One will
contain retail sales information. The other will contain
wholesale information.

You can see the children's book retail catalog page here -
*http://www.sybrina.com/index_Sybrina_Publishing_Children_
Stories_Retail_Catalog.htm*

I don't include a link to this from any other page on my website
but here's the children's book wholesale catalog page. It
contains links to wholesale information for the books which
have been published through LightningSource. It used to also
have links to the CreateSpace pages for each of my books with
discount codes but sadly, CreateSpace has discontinued that
amazing service for authors to offer to customers.

This wholesale link on your website can be sent to stores or gift
shops along with other wholesale marketing material.

*http://www.sybrina.com/index_Sybrina_Publishing_Children_
Stories_Wholesale_Catalog.htm*

One of the most important pages on your website will be the
webpage dedicated to your book. There you will have the
ability to place all of the information which you feel is most
important about the book. It's also where you can link to every
single online book seller you can find who is offering your book
for sale. As humongous as Amazon is, the fact is apparent, for
whatever reason, not everyone wants to purchase books from
them so help your potential customers find your book where
ever it might reside on the internet. If you've branched out and
are also publishing through IngramSpark, you'll want to list the
Barnes and Noble books links and the epub book links on your
book webpage, too.

Note: *About a month after your book has been published on
Amazon and again after it's been published for a month or so
through IngramSpark, do a Google search on "Buy Your Book
Title". Click on every link that comes up. Copy and paste that
online store's link into the book's page on your website or blog.
I kid you not...you may be in for some surprises. I even found*

one of my books, "Yarashell Abbily and Her Very Messy Room" online at Walmart!

In 2015 it showed that it was out of stock and there was no way to place an order but I was able to sign up to receive a notification email when it is "back in stock". Now, in 2017, there is a purchase link, not only for this book but for all of my books! Whoo-hoo! I guess Walmart is trying their hardest to compete with Amazon for online sales.

See it here - **https://www.walmart.com/ip/Yarashell-Abbily-and-Her-Very-Messy-Room/41675236**

Here is the feature book page for "Yarashell Abbily and Her Very Messy Room on my website...with the link to the Walmart page in the upper left corner along with all the other online stores!

http://www.sybrina.com/index_Yarashell_Abbily_and_Her_Very_Messy_Room_Book_Info.htm

Here's another sample of one of my feature book pages –

http://www.sybrina.com/index_Rabbit_Fox_Story_Listen_To_Song_For_Free.htm.

You will also want to include a link on the book's website page to a sample chapter of your book. The last page of the sample should include a link for purchasing the book.

Example of the last page of a reading sample.

Finish reading this book with your child!

It is available in
Kindle and epub
ebook formats
and in
soft cover and hard back.
The hardback makes a
great forever keepsake.

Find out where to get it in your favorite formats at

http://www.sybrina.com/index_Nellie_Knows_How_To_Knot_A_Neck_Scarf.htm

Listen to the accompanying song there for FREE, also.

PS: If you would like to read this book to your child and are low on funds, ask your local children's librarian to purchase it in Hard Cover format - ISBN # 978-0-9906537-7-6 (8 ½ x 11) so that you can finish reading it for free.

Below is a sample of a book page on my website. All of
the links at the upper left go directly to my book page at online
book stores other than Amazon.

I personally like to create and publish my website using
Microsoft Publisher because it is so easy to use. It is basically a
program that allows you to drag and drop images where ever
you want them to appear on a webpage. It's easy to add links
to other pages within your website and to other places on the
internet. And it's super easy to add html codes for widgets for
selling your books through your Amazon Associate account,
among other things.

If you use Microsoft Publisher you will need a web host provider
and an FTP program for uploading your website files to the
webhost. I use ***http://www.doteasy.com/*** to host my websites.
They will also secure your website domain name for you. They
are very easy to deal with and very reasonably priced. The FTP
program I use is Ipswitch WS_FTP. I highly recommend you
check out Doteasy.com and ***http://www.ipswitchft.com/ws-***

ftp-client but there are many other similar services available. Choose what works the best for you.

If you don't want to take the time to learn all about those things there are lots of online options available for blogs and websites. You can set up a simple free website or blog through WordPress.com (*https://wordpress.com/*). They also offer upgraded abilities for a fee. Network Solutions (*http://www.networksolutions.com/*) is a great low priced and fairly easy to use website or blog creator and host. Both of these web hosts will register your website domain name for you.

Paid Book Promotion Sites

There are so many places to pay for book promotion that it will make your head spin when you start researching. Many authors swear by Amazon paid ads only. Others use Facebook post boosts exclusively. There are many Twitter services which will tweet about your books to their massive audiences. And there are sites where readers go to look for books. Some of the biggest sites are listed below:

https://www.bookbub.com

http://awesomegang.com/submit-your-book/

http://librarybub.com/authors/

https://www.booksbutterfly.com/

https://bookgoodies.com/submit-your-free-kindle-days/highlight-your-free-kindle-days/

https://thebookpromoter.com/

https://www.bargainbooksy.com/for-authors/

https://booksgosocial.com/

https://www.thekindlebookreview.net/advertising/

The following is not a book promotion site but it does offer a handy tool for you to keep track of sites you have used. *https://www.readersintheknow.com/list-of-book-promotion-sites*

Interestingly enough, many of these book promotional sites will not market your book unless you already have a certain number of reviews on Amazon. Seems really unfair doesn't it? What to do?????

Another thing about book promotions sites is that many of them will only promote your "FREE" ebook. Now, you may be thinking, "I want to sell books, not give them away!" But sometimes you have to give in order to receive. For instance, if you have written a series of 3 books, you might want to give the first one away for free in order to hook your readers.

The reality is – some of the people who read your free book will become new fans and will want to read your other books and some won't. Many readers who download free ebooks never even read them. With this in mind, you need to weigh all possible effects on you personally before you decide to go this route.

For me, I'm actually giving away The Blue Unicorn's Journey To Osm Illustrated Book For Teens and Older Readers in ebook format to everyone who subscribes to my newsletter. I figure, if they love it, they might actually want to purchase the printed book as a collectible or as a gift for someone else. Who knows, I might even get some nice book reviews out of the deal.

To see how truly mind-boggling the amount of resources there are who offer books to readers for free, check out this article on the subject - *https://www.thebalance.com/places-to-get-free-kindle-books-1357954*

Paid Book Reviews

People will tell you that it's inappropriate to pay for book reviews. To that, I say, "WHAT!??????!" Though many words have been written on the subject, nearly every publisher or author ends up paying for reviews in some manner or other. Some, in combination with their advertising efforts in certain publications; some by paying "marketing" services to promote their books for them; and others by outright paying for outrageously expensive reviews from such renowned publications as Kirkus or Clarion.

OK, since the idea of paid book reviews seems to offend so many people in the publishing industry; to make people feel better about the subject, let's just call it Paid Book Publicity from this point forward.

If you decide to pay for reviews (paid book publicity), make sure you have researched the site where your review (paid book publicity) will be posted. If you have a good feeling about it, then by all means, go for it. One important point about paid reviews (paid book publicity)...until the mindset changes, be very careful about where those reviews are posted. Amazon and Goodreads (who happen to be affiliated with each other) are both very picky about allowing what they perceive to be paid reviews (paid book publicity) on their sites.

They will literally scan sites offering book review services and they will ding you for allowing those sites to post on Amazon or Goodreads. They will even hide or erase reviews that they feel were gathered inappropriately. It is very disturbing to note but they have been known to take extremely negative measures

against people (and their books) who they have determined
paid for reviews (paid book publicity) that appear on their sites.

My advice is to only pay for reviews which will appear on a book
bloggers site or a book review website because you don't want
to chance being banned from Goodreads or having your
Amazon reviews deleted. It has happened to far too many
independent authors, who in my opinion, don't deserve such
shabby treatment. Although most paid reviews (paid book
publicity) are pretty expensive, there are some book reviewers
who provide relatively inexpensive book reviews. Here's a good
article on the subject.
*https://www.emptymirrorbooks.com/publishing/10-ways-to-
find-reviewers-for-your-self-published-book*

Here is a link to some different reviewers -
http://www.tweetyourbooks.com/p/free-reviews.html.

Do some internet research on "Book Reviewers" or "Book
Review Services" to find others. Many have their own blogs or
websites, Facebook pages or other places where they will post
the reviews. As mentioned before, avoid purchasing from
reviewers who state they will post on Amazon or GoodReads.
You need to look for reviewers who state they will post on their
own blog.

There is a lot of value in acquiring some reviews. One of the
most valuable reasons is that it makes it more likely for your
book to be found by strangers doing internet searches. Links to
these reviews on blogs and other sources may also be added to
your own website book review page. It gives people who land
there lots of opportunities for seeing others people opinions of
your book. One other thing to note...not every free or paid
review will be a 5 or even 4 star review but there is nothing
wrong with that. There is no one book in the world that will
ever be perfect for everyone. Here are some reviews of my
unicorn book.

http://www.sybrinablueunicornbook.com/index_Blue_Unicorn _Book_Reviews.htm

Virtual Book Publicity Tours

A virtual book publicity tour typically consists of your book making a circuit among book bloggers who inform others about your book via reviews, author interviews, guest posts and more. The "tour" is typically advertised by the book tour hosting company and also by the individual bloggers who have signed up to interview you or review your book on the tour. Nothing is ever really guaranteed but your interviews could possibly end up being published in major magazines and newspapers. The price range for these publicity packages run from just under $200.00 to potentially thousands of dollars.

You can learn more about some different virtual tours here –

http://www.pumpupyourbook.com/about-us/

http://www.goddessfish.com/

https://bewitchingbooktours.blogspot.com/

http://silver-dagger-scriptorium.weebly.com/book-tours

http://xpressobooktours.com/services/

http://tlcbooktours.com/

http://yaboundbooktours.blogspot.com/p/services.html

http://www.rockstarbooktours.com/

http://www.b00kr3vi3ws.in/p/services.html - They are from India but many of the tour hosts are in the US and other places around the world.

https://audiobookwormpromotions.com/tours/

Twitter Pitch Parties

Many blogs sponsor something called Twitter Pitch Parties. These are events offering opportunities to pitch manuscripts to industry professionals. Some Twitter hashtags to follow are #Adpit (for pitching adult books) and #Kidpit (for pitching kids books). The only roadblock...the pitch may not be longer than 140 charactersSome blogs to check out are below:

http://writerswow.blogspot.com/2014/01/wwow-get-your-pitch-on-twitter-pitch.html

https://twitter.com/pitchmas

http://www.brenda-drake.com/contest-schedule

https://slushpilestory.wordpress.com/2017/11/04/most-popular-twitter-pitch-parties-for-writers/

If you do a search on "virtual book publicity tours" or "twitter pitch parties", you can learn more than you ever imagined about services offered by many different companies.

Press Releases

It is important to let the public know about your book with a well written press release. Sometimes press releases are picked up by journalists who will use it to give emphasis to a particular subject. If they happen to work for a major newspaper or magazine (physical or online) or even for radio or television then the chances of people learning of your book increase greatly.

Also, once your press release has been published online, it will have a permanent place on the World Wide Web. My advice is to immediately copy the link to your published press release and place that link on your own blog or website so that you can point people there for further publicity purposes.

See some of my press releases at
http://www.sybrina.com/index_Press_Releases_for_Learn_To _Tie_A_Tie_With_The_Rabbit_And_The_Fox.htm.

It's difficult to find Free Press Release submission services. If you do a search on Google, you will find plenty of "lists" of Free Press Release sites. Let me warn you that most of them are not really free. That's why my preferred service is Fiverr.com. You'll find people there who will write a press release for you for $5.00 and others who will submit press releases for you for $5.00 per service.

Just make certain that you only select the services that say they submit to sites like PRBuzz, SB Wire, PRNewswire, AP, Google News and such. Those are professional press release sites which charge hundreds of dollars a year to each customer for use of their services. Fiverr.com press release service providers typically purchase yearly subscriptions on those sites making it financially viable for them to submit hundreds or even thousands of press releases per year for customers who hire them on Fiverr. It is a great service for those of us who don't have thousands of $$$ to spend on yearly subscriptions.

There are also service providers on Fiverr and elsewhere who will post your press release on large Facebook and Twitter accounts. Some of those might be worthwhile, while many will not be. Use your good judgment before spending your money.

I have also used a service that specializes in Book Press Releases. It is a little more expensive but you will definitely get a few book reviews out of their efforts. If you have a hundred bucks to spend on a one time release, Bostick Communications is definitely one to go with.

Check them out at *http://www.bostickcommunications.com*

HARO (Help A Reporter Out) – This is a unique way to get some press for your book. You can sign up with this site to become a "reporter". They will send frequent emails listing the needs of different newspapers, magazines, television new programs and more by subject. If you feel you are an expert on any given subject matter, especially if the subject relates to your book, then submit an article to them for that subject. Your article might just be the one selected for publication and since your book will be mentioned in the byline, that provides an excellent opportunity for complete strangers to click the link to purchase it. How's that for free advertising?

Check them out here - *http://www.helpareporter.com/*

ARTICLE PUBLISHING SITES

There are also sites where you may submit articles for publication. As long as you use good grammar and follow their rules, they will usually post your article on its own webpage. You could potentially utilize these services as a sort of press release site. What you would do is write an article relevant to the subject matter of your book and post a link to your free book sample pdf file or to a page on your website in the credits. You would also link back to the article from your website, your blog, Facebook and any other place you wish. Check out the article publishing sites listed below:

http://ezinearticles.com/

http://www.articleworld.org/index.php/Main_Page

http://www.amazines.com/

http://www.ezine-dir.com/

http://hubpages.com/

There are quite a few more but this is more than enough to get
you started. I told you promoting your book would be a lot of
work! Promoting songs is a lot of work, too. Check out the
articles I wrote and posted for 2 of my songs.

*http://ezinearticles.com/?So,-You-Say-Youre-Getting-
Married?-Remember-It-Takes-Two-To-Tango!&id=5065967*

and

*http://ezinearticles.com/?Why-Little-Girls-Love-Big-
Dresses&id=5114254*

Book Expos and Craft Fairs

There are many services offering to take your book with them
to book fairs all over the world. Book fairs target regional,
national and international buyers from retailers to libraries.
Some of the biggest ones are Book Expo America, Frankfurt
International Book Fair and the American Library Association
Annual. There are literally hundreds of book fairs held every
year. For a pretty large fee, these services promise to expose
your book to the thousands of attendees at any given show.
Most will also offer an online profile listing of your book for a
year. And all offer some kind of discount for bulk titles and
multiple shows. Some will even send you a mailing list with
names of people who attended the shows, which you can send
post cards and other promotional materials to.

Other than that, I'm not really certain I am convinced of the
value of these services because your book will be just one of
hundreds sitting on the shelves of each exhibitor at these

shows. Also, there's no way that all of any one shows attendees will see your book, much less pick it up to browse through it. But there is always hope that yours will stand out in the crowd so you might consider this a potentially good marketing option.

Here are some for you to check out for yourself.

http://www.globalbookshows.com/

http://www.combinedbook.com/

https://publishers.forewordreviews.com/trade-shows/

http://www.bookmarketingprofits.com/TradeShows.html

A Related Problem To Consider

One real problem you've probably never thought you'd have to deal with is what to do with an over abundance of printed books.

In addition to the book expos mentioned above, you might also want to participate in book fairs or events like craft shows, kid's shows, Holiday markets and the like.

You will need to have inventory for any of these events and you might not sell out all of your books. That's not where the real problem comes in, though, because you can always try to sell them again...unless you decide to make some changes to your book.

What do you do if you've ordered a bunch of copies of your book and they are no longer the final word on your subject? Never fear – You can always bring them to the next fair or craft show and offer them at a highly discounted rate in a bargain bin.

You might also want to take them somewhere like Half Price Books or other book co-ops and possibly sell them for a few cents on the dollar. That way your investment wouldn't be a total loss.

On a loftier note, you could donate them to hospitals and other charities such as women's shelters. They would be greatly appreciated in those places and it's more likely that they will receive a wider reading audience than they might in a used book store.

You can also send them out as Beta or Review copies but whatever you do with these early versions of your books, make certain that you add a note to the inside cover that "editing issues have been addressed in the final edition". Use a stick on label to ensure your message doesn't get lost. Prefix your note text to say something like "Uncorrected Proof Copy". This will ensure that no one thinks the book is the final copy of your work.

Book Reader (and Author) Websites

There are lots of book promotion websites out there. Most purport to have thousands of reader subscribers to whom they send daily or weekly book promotion emails. Some of them offer onetime payment options for authors and others want you to purchase monthly subscriptions for book promotion services. Some offer the opportunity for you to offer giveaways of your books. And some offer free books to potential reviewers. Of course the books will be provided by the author, not the site.

Goodreads Giveaways - *You can offer your book for a Giveaway on GoodReads. There are 2 packages. The standard package costs authors $119 to give away up to 100 copies. The premium package will cost $599, but it will give your book giveaway an exclusive placement on its Giveaways page. Both the standard*

*and premium packages will automatically add a contest book to
each entrant's Want-To-Read list. Also, users who have already
added the book to the Want-To-Read list will be notified if it's
the subject of a contest. Goodreads used to only allow printed
book giveaways but now if your book is in the Kindle Unlimited
program you can giveaway ebooks.*

*Remember, whether your giveaway is for a print or ebook, you
will have to purchase the books you are giving away. For
printed books you will have to pay shipping costs. You can
purchase the print books from your CreateSpace account for less
than wholesale cost and to save money on mailing out printed
books, you can send them to winners directly from your
CreateSpace account.*

*To list a Goodreads giveaway, you will need to log in to your
Goodreads account. Once there, go to the page for the book
and click "List Giveaway".*

By the way…Amazon now offers giveaway opportunities for
authors. Just as with Goodreads or any other giveaway for that
matter, you, the author will have to purchase your own book to
send to the winner. In this case, though, you actually have to
purchase it from Amazon at retail price. You will also pay for
shipping to the winner and pay a fee for Amazon to set up your
giveaway page. They will provide you with a link to your
giveaway and you can share that link on Facebook and all other
social media sites that you are associated with. Is it worth it?
Only you can decide but it might generate some additional buzz
for your book. Use this link to access the Amazon giveaway
page.

https://www.amazon.com/gp/giveaway/home

http://www.booklemur.com/ - Readers can even easily read
books downloaded from this site on their smart phones.

http://www.freado.com/ - This service is free for readers but they are associated with BookBuzzr.com which is not free to Authors who want to utilize their advertising feature.

https://readersfavorite.com/ - They offer book reviews and an international book award contest. They also have an Author Book Donation Program. Through it, authors may promise to send copies of their books to needy schools, libraries and foundations.

http://firstchapterplus.com/ - This site features an online catalog of books as well as monthly emails to readers. They distribute their catalog to libraries, independent book stores, media, readers, other writers, bloggers and reviewers.

http://www.bookdaily.com/bdconnect - Another site for connecting authors and readers through their featured Author of the Day newsletter.

http://www.ebookbooster.com/ - They offer to promote your ebook to about 45 reading sites. They also list sites which you may submit your books to yourself for free.

If you are interested in offering your ebooks for free or at serious discounted prices, this website offers a list of many places where you can sign up to do so.

https://www.thebalance.com/places-to-get-free-kindle-books-1357954

Newsletter Swap Services

If you have been collecting email addresses from people who are interested in your books and you make use of a newsletter distribution service, then you will be interested in newsletter swap services. These are opportunities for authors who have mailing lists to take turns promoting each other's books to their email subscribers. This is a great way for each author to gain new subscribers who are interested in their books and hopefully to gain many new book fans and sales. Some are free to join and most require that you have at least 100 or more subscribers.

Some to try are

http://bookhub.online/authors-news/newsletter-swap-suggestions

https://www.bookboast.com/

https://authorsxp.com/for-authors/author-newsletter-swap

https://www.tckpublishing.com/author-email-list-swap-application/

You can also find a lot of newsletter swappers on Facebook. Just search for "newsletter swap".

Advertising in Search Engines

If you have a website or blog you might want to consider "pay per click" advertising with a Google adwords account. There are also many different types of advertising on other search engines.

The way that "pay per click" works is you create a text or picture ad containing a hyperlink to your webpage. When someone does a search for the keywords related to your ad, then your ad will appear on the right side of the search pages as a paid advertisement. If anyone clicks on your ad, you will be charged the price that you bid for your key word(s). The more popular a

key word is, the more Google charges you for it. So, their
advertising can become very expensive very quickly.

Learn more about Google adwords at
http://www.google.com/adwords/ .

A more reasonably priced alternative is Exactseek.com. They
offer pay per click ads at a fraction of the cost of adwords.

Learn more about them at *https://store.exactseek.com/*.

Goodreads, Amazon and Facebook all offer pay per click
advertising, too.

Create and Give Away or Better Yet - Sell Merchandise Based On Your Book

Unfortunately not everyone will purchase your book from a
book fair or craft show even if they are really, really interested
in it. Many would just rather buy the ebook later. So how do
you get them to remember your book.   You do so with what's
called "Book Bling" or "Book Swag" or "Book Loot".

Those are terms used for items specifically created to promote a
book. Most authors don't have a lot of money to spend so they
might just have book marks and post cards printed that have a
picture of the book on one side and information about the book
on the other. These can be great memory joggers for people
who want to buy your book later.

There are many online printers who offer great deals on those
items. VistaPrint.com and PrintRunner.com are just two. Do a
search and you will find many more.

They will print stickers too, but ***https://www.stickeryou.com/***
might have more options than they do. Plus they offer iron-ons
and temporary tattoos! Have your book cover or logo or quote
from the book printed on a sticker that can be placed on a
binder or other hard surface and your book will be
remembered.

Another cool offering for your potential customers are rubber
bracelets. They can be printed with your Facebook page
address or your website address or just the name of your book
in some cool font. Find them and many other attention
grabbing items at ***https://www.wrist-band.com/*** .

Customized pens make great giveaway reminders. Pencils are
ok too but they don't come in all the unique styles then pens
do. The best place to get them is ***http://www.pens.com/*** .

All of the above items can be given away to fans of your books.
You could sell them, too, but not everyone has the ability to
create, stock and deliver these types of items all over creation.
That's where sites like Zazzle.com come in. They make it a
breeze to offer book bling products to interested customers.

It is completely free for you to upload graphic images that you
have designed for marketing and promoting your book to
Zazzle.com.   You can associate the graphic image to any
product (book marks, posters, t-shirts, jewelry, coffee mugs,
trading cards and so much more!) that is available on their site.
And the best part of all is that if the item sells, you will get a
small commission from the sale. Just look at some of the book
related things I offer in my Journey To Osm Collection on Zazzle.
***https://www.zazzle.com/collections/journey_to_osm-
119557554153312638***

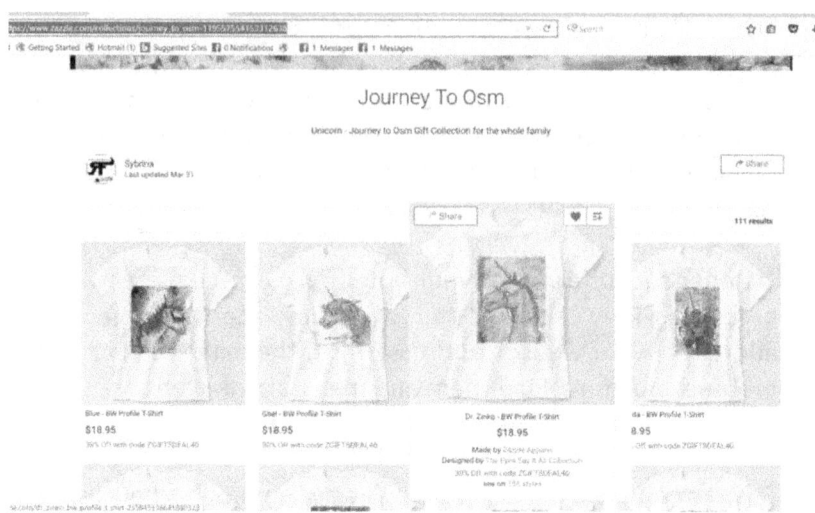

If you think it's a great idea to promote your book with Book
Bling, go to *www.zazzle.com* and click on the "Sell on Zazzle"
link to learn more about setting up your own store.

When you start adding your designs to products you will notice
that the products sell for more than they would at other big box
stores but remember; your designs are unique and your
potential customers will not be able to find these one of a kind
items with images from your book anywhere else. Also, Zazzle
offers site wide sales all the time. When you know one is
occurring, that is a good time to place sale notices on your
social media.

I use Zazzle almost exclusively but there are other sites that are
just as good or maybe even better.

One of oldest is *www.Cafepress.com* Just click the "Start
Selling" button to learn more about selling there.

Some others are *https://www.spreadshirt.com/* ,
https://www.designbyhumans.com/ ,and
https://society6.com/.

If you are really creative and can make 3D design drawings, *https://www.shapeways.com* is a great site for you to check out. You can upload your plans and have 3D products created in plastic, ceramic, stainless steel and many other mediums.

More About Book Loot

Readers are cashing in on the craze of book box purchases via lots of different distributors of Book Loot, Swag or Bling. Some of these companies say they will feature Indie Author books in their boxes. So, it won't hurt to contact a few to see if your book is appealing enough for them to do so.

http://www.hootlootbox.com

https://www.fairyloot.com

https://www.cratejoy.com/sell/

https://www.uppercasebox.com

https://quarterlyhq.wufoo.com/forms/partner-with-quarterly/

http://www.thebookdrop.com/about

https://litjoycrate.com/vendors

https://www.bookishboxinfo.com/faq

http://mybookbox.com/faq#2

https://www.bookofthemonth.com/contact-us - There's no bling or loot in these boxes but this is the official "book of the month club" so here is where you can try to get your book selected for inclusion.

There are many more book loot services so do a search on "book box subscription" and get busy researching and contacting them. And if you've managed to build up your newsletter subscriber list to sky-high proportions, consider offering your own custom book boxes to customers who purchase box sets or hardback copies of your books.

Online Giveaways

Online giveaways are a great way to build your mailing lists. A great giveaway prize is an autographed copy of your book. If you are giving away a printed copy of your book, I would suggest that you only allow entrants from the United States or the country that you live in. Postage fees can be very expensive when mailing parcels overseas or to other countries.

There are several online services that are great for hosting online contests. Some are

https://www.rafflecopter.com

https://promosimple.com/

https://gleam.io/app/competitions

https://www.viralsweep.com/pricing

https://www.shortstack.com

After you've set up your giveaway, how in the world do you get out the word about your contest?

Most of the online giveaway companies listed above have viral forms you can embed in your website or your Facebook fan page. You can do a boosted post about it on Facebook or on Twitter.

You can also use giveaway announcement services. Some of the ones listed below are free and some require you add a badge to their site but others have upgraded perks that cost a few bucks like listing your contest in their newsletter or posting about it lots of times on their social networks. Some good ones are:

http://www.hypersweep.com/

http://www.giveawaypromote.com/

http://giveawayfrenzy.com/giveaway-submit/

http://www.infinitesweeps.com/submit/

https://www.contestalley.com

Here's a good list of contest promotion sites. *https://upviral.com/100-contest-promotion-websites/* Just do a search on "giveaway announcement sites" to find tons more.

You can also find some useful resources for promoting your giveaways on Fiverr.com and Facebook. Just search for "Promote Giveaway" on those sites to find them.

Get Funding For Your Project

If you simply do not have the money to engage in any of the paid services listed above, do not feel that there's no hope for you. There are a myriad of opportunities for you to gain financial interest in your project through rewards crowd funding. To do this, you would pre-sell a product (your book) to launch publishing or promotional efforts without incurring

future debt. If you haven't heard of any before, some of the
most popular internet based crowd funding sites are

www.Indiegogo.com

www.crowdfunder.com

www.Kickstarter.com

www.GoFundMe.com

www.Razoo.com

www.Crowdrise.com

All of these sites charge fees but you could get away with paying
out as little as 3% of what you raise to around 5%. Some charge
a monthly fee and others charge credit card fees so do your
homework before selecting the best option for you. You will
find many other crowd funding and angel investing sources out
there; some even interested in books with a non-profit or
charitable slant.

Now there's something new that's being referred to as "Crowd
Speaking". It's a new tool for authors called Thunderclap.
Supposedly, it's like an online flash mob that lets you and others
share the same message at the same time, spreading an idea
through Facebook, Twitter, and Tumblr. Currently, it is still free
so if you're interested read about it at
https://www.thunderclap.it/

Educate Yourself

Educate Yourself For FREE

Now that you've started educating yourself about book
formatting, publishing and marketing; don't stop here. There
are myriad of ways to educate yourself for FREE. A simple
search on the internet will bring up links to more articles than
you'll ever have time to read. Search for key words like writing
tips or groups, publishing tips or groups, print on demand,
reader groups, book publicity or anything else you're curious
about. One link will lead to others and in time your knowledge
base will expand far beyond what you ever thought possible.

Speaking of reader groups, check out ***https://www.scribd.com/***
. This is a great place to post articles about your book with links
to a free pdf reading sample. Or you can even post the free
reading sample directly on the site.

If you prefer opportunities to get out and meet with real
people, check your public library's calendar for events for
writers or even readers. Also, many writers' clubs have their
own websites. Look on the internet for local writers or readers
groups that you can join. One of the best sites for finding
groups of people with your interests who spend time with each
other regularly is Meetup.com. If you don't find what you're
looking for, you can always start a group of your own and list it
there for others to find.

One of the very best educational and business sites is LinkedIn.
There, you can join all kinds of groups to participate in. LinkedIn
gives you the option to create a company page and product
pages from your personal account page. If you already have a
LinkedIn profile for your "regular" career and don't want your
writing persona to be associated with the real you, you can try
setting up another account with a pen name and a different
email address.

But the very bad news is LinkedIn only allows one account per individual. Do not use the same exact name for your author account that you have on your other career account because if they find out that you have 2 accounts, they will lock you out of one of them. I know because it happened to me. They locked me out of my account that I had set up to gain contacts in the writing and publishing world. No amount of pleading or reasoning could sway them to my point of view on the subject. So, if you would like to link up with me, please don't let the fact that you will be linking up with my alter ego in the oil and gas industry dissuade you from contacting me.

Look me up on LinkedIn here -
https://www.linkedin.com/pub/sybrina-durant/18/772/509

Also, feel free to visit and "like" my company page there –

https://www.linkedin.com/company/sybrina-publishing

Publishing Organizations

Consider spending a little bit of money joining some publishing organizations. I highly recommend the Independent Book Publishers Association (IBPA). As a member, you'll get a monthly magazine in your snail mail box. I personally love holding a magazine in my hand so that I can fold over the corners of pages that I want to remember. I refer to these over and over again.

They also offer some fantastic paid services for author/publishers such as Library Eblasts, Books For Review Catalog, Book Store Catalog plus opportunities to enter your book into different Awards programs. You can also pay to have them represent your book at industry trade shows like BEA Expo, American Library Association Annual Conference and the Frankfurt Book Fair.

Learn more about IBPA at ***http://www.ibpa-
online.org/page/membership***

IBPA is not the only valuable source of education for writers.
There are many writers organizations geared specifically to
particular genres.

For instance, there's the Romance Writers of America
(***https://www.rwa.org/***),

the Society of Children's Book Writers and Illustrators
(***http://www.scbwi.org/***)

the Science Fiction and Fantasy Writers of America
(***https://www.sfwa.org/***),

the Garden Writers Association (***http://gardenwriters.org***) and

an organization for recipe journalists – The International
Association of Culinary Professionals
(**https://www.iacp.com/awards/cookbook/**). They even have
cookbook awards contests.

And there's the Mystery Writers of America
(***https://mysterywriters.org/***)
just to name a few.

Audio book publishers have an organization also
(**https://www.audiopub.org/**)

A quick search on the internet can introduce you to writing
groups for nearly every type of book. And the best part of it all
is that you can join and interact with these organizations online.

There are also some great writer education websites that I
recommend. One is the Author Marketing Club. They have a

very informative catalog of videos for many different aspects of
book producing, publishing and promotion at

http://authormarketingclub.com/members/checklist/.

http://spawn.org/ - SPAWN stands for Small Publishers, Artists
& Writers Network. You will find lots of great information and
opportunities here for authors and publishers. It costs less than
$100.00 a year to be a member.

http://www.bookweb.org/ - This is the website for the
American Booksellers Association which is mainly geared
towards professional book sellers like book stores. However
publishers may become associate members.   ABA also "rents"
its ABA bookstore mailing list. This could be a very useful list if
you are going to be sending out postcards or fliers about your
books to stores.

Another fantastic site for writer resources is
*http://www.nownovel.com/blog/151-important-novel-
writing-resources/* . They list everything from baby name
generators to romance universities.

Even if you decide not to spend any money joining any of these
organizations, look around the websites to see if you can sign
up for free newsletters. Sometimes the little tidbits of
information they provide are worth their weight in gold.

Finally, if you find yourself struggling with writer's block and just
can't think of the right way to describe something, check out
http://www.phrasethesaurus.com .

Libraries and WorldCat.org

WorldCat.org is the world's largest network of library content
and services. It is a library catalog designed to help you find

library materials online. It is mainly updated by public and school librarians who use this service to list all of the books on the shelves of their library but anyone who has an interest can join to review and rate books.

After you've spent a bit of time marketing and promoting your book you'll want to check *http://www.worldcat.org/*to see if your book happens to be "shelved" at any libraries. Go to the WorldCat website to do a search by author name and you'll see all of the books listed there for that author. Click on one of the book links to see all of the libraries which have placed that book on their bookshelves and registered it with WorldCat.

It is very difficult but not impossible for self-published authors to convince a librarian to shelve their book.

For instance, visit the public library in your area and ask the librarian there if they will shelve it. Make certain that you've listed the BISAC codes on the upper left of the back book cover and inside on the Copyright page as discussed in the beginning of this instruction document. That will increase the possibility for your book to be shelved.

Most libraries have websites. If you don't do well "going door to door" for personal sales visits, log on to all the libraries that you can find that allow you to get a "temporary" library card at their branch. Once you receive your temporary card number, you can click on the "Submit Book" link and request that the librarian purchase your book. Have all of your information ready, in a Word doc or notepad, for copying and pasting into the online form.

In addition to your book title, BISAC codes (genre), age group, ISBN number (hardback only for children's books) and number of pages, you should also provide a link in the notes section to your books free pdf sample. If your ebook is available on

Overdrive.com, you should definitely mention that. Also include the link to your books "wholesale page" on your website.

Keep a spreadsheet to log all of the libraries you have submitted your book to. Frequently check, worldcat.org to see if your efforts are paying off. By the way, some librarians will actually email you to say they are going to purchase your book. Make sure you thank them profusely.

For children's books, make sure you offer the librarian a hard back, not a paperback because children are very hard on library books. Librarians typically will not shelve a paperback because they become tattered so quickly. Another thing that librarians prefer is a book with the title on the spine. Unfortunately, it is not always possible to get the printer to print on the spine of a very thin book these days but try to get that done if at all possible.

Remember too, that many librarians attend book fairs and many actually purchase books for their libraries from those offered at the fairs.

And then of course, through CreateSpace, Ingram Spark and many other distributors, there is a possibility that a librarian may see your book in a catalog and purchase it for their library.

Finally, check out ***http://self-e.libraryjournal.com/*** . In their own words, "SELF-e enables you to make your ebook available to thousands of readers via participating public libraries in your state, and offers the potential to reach a much larger national audience via Library Journal's curated collections." It is free for independent self-published authors to submit published books for the opportunity to be shelved at libraries all over the country. PDF and Epub files are accepted.

Final Thoughts

There are so many more aspects of producing, publishing and promoting books that I have not covered in this instruction book. Honestly, a book with everything in it would be thousands of pages long. But I have given you enough information in a little less than 200 pages for you to successfully present your book to the public for sale and to jump right into marketing it.

I am very interested in your thoughts about the information I've provided. Oh sure, I'm well aware that I've done a lot of shameless promotion in nearly every section of this book but hey, I'm sharing my personal experience with you so it's only natural to show you samples of my work. And you can believe I want to see samples of yours once you have published your book.

Please feel **FREE** to write to me at Sybrina@sybrina.com with questions, comments or suggestions.

Along the way, I'd love to hear about your journey with your book. And when you need a little extra inspiration to be motivated, listen to my song, "Help Yourself" at my website for free! Here's link - *http://www.phrasethesaurus.com/HelpYourself-8-7-2015.mp3* The lyrics are on the next page to make it easy for you to sing along.

Hear most of my songs for free on various pages at my website, *http://www.sybrina.com* .

Lyrics for Help Yourself

Verse 1
The best place to find a helping hand
is on the end of your own arm.
Success can be at your command
If you believe in number one.

Chorus
Help yourself
and you will go far.
Believe in your capacity
to reach the highest star.
Think of all the possibilities
to make your dreams reality.
No one can do
what you can do for yourself.

Verse 2
The best place to find a helping hand
is on the end of your own arm.
No victory is sweeter than
knowing that you've left your mark.

Repeat Chorus

Bridge
You've gotta believe....
You've gotta believe in yourself.
You've gotta believe....
You've gotta believe in yourself
cause no one can do
what you can do for yourself.

Repeat Chorus

About the Author

Who is Sybrina Durant and what are her qualifications for
writing this book?

Well, truly, I'm pretty much a nobody. I'm not a sought after
public figure or a captain of industry. If you passed me on the
street, you probably wouldn't notice. And to tell you the truth, I
like it that way. Passing through social situations incognito has
it perks.

I don't have a college degree. But I do have an inordinate
amount of life experience and an extreme drive to accomplish
anything I set my mind to. Sadly, most of those interests
involve intellectual pursuits of some kind. If I were the same
way with physical activities, all the other ladies might be
jealous...but wolf whistles are now just echoes from my past.

I'm a firm a believer in the "teach a man to fish" philosophy. A
man who can catch his own meal will never go hungry.   I'm
totally agreeable with the concept of a safety net to catch
someone who falls but I don't like the idea of offering someone
a lifelong hammock in which to lazily loll around the rest of their
life. For me, the younger a person learns and implements a
skill, the better.

Researching, gathering and compiling knowledge brings me joy.
I love to learn and I love to share what I've learned with others.
I believe everyone has something of value to share. If they just
give it some thought, they'll figure it out. With the proper
motivation and tools, they can enlighten their own sphere of
influence and maybe even the world beyond.

That is the reason for this book. I spent a lot of time gathering
the necessary knowledge for me to produce, publish and
promote my books, as well as those of my sister, my friend, my

mother-in-law and even the one I published posthumously for my Dad.

I'm far from a know it all…but I do know a bunch of stuff and I learned it all on my own. That's what makes me qualified to write this book. I "Helped Myself" to all of the knowledge available to me. I didn't sit around boo-hoo-hooing that no one would help me or that nobody cared. I just did it and you can, too.

The information in this book was gathered along my personal journey in publishing. It is filled with my personal experiences that got me to this point. You may already know some of the things in it. You may disagree with some of the things in it because you did it another way and that's o.k. because as they say, "There's more than one way to skin a cat".

Or this entire process may be totally new for you. Either way, I hope I've shared something you feel is valuable for your own personal journey and that you use it in the pursuit of your dreams.

Visit my Pinterest pages often for more inspiration to Help Yourself achieve your writing and publishing goals.

https://www.pinterest.com/sybrinad/help-yourself/

and

https://www.pinterest.com/sybrinad/sybrinas-phrase-thesaurus/